CLINGING
TO THE
VINE

Reflections for Cultivating
a Fruitful *and* Connected Life

By

MEGAN CARLTON

Foreword by

BETH JOHNSON

Published by hope*books
2217 Matthews Township Pkwy
Suite D302
Matthews, NC 28105
www.hopebooks.com

hope*books is a division of hope*media

Printed in the United States of America

First paperback edition.
Paperback ISBN: 979-8-89185-290-7
Hardcover ISBN: 979-8-89185-291-4
Ebook ISBN: 979-8-89185-292-1
Library of Congress Number: 2025943350

Scripture quotations marked (NLT) are taken from the Holy Bible, New Living Translation, copyright ©1996, 2004, 2015 by Tyndale House Foundation. Used by permission of Tyndale House Publishers, Carol Stream, Illinois 60188. All rights reserved.

Scripture quotations marked (NIV) are taken from the Holy Bible, New International Version®, NIV®. Copyright © 1973, 1978, 1984, 2011 by Biblica, Inc.™ Used by permission of Zondervan. All rights reserved worldwide. www.zondervan.comThe "NIV" and "New International Version" are trademarks registered in the United States Patent and Trademark Office by Biblica, Inc.™

Scripture quotations marked TPT are from The Passion Translation®. Copyright © 2017, 2018, 2020 by Passion & Fire Ministries, Inc. Used by permission. All rights reserved. ThePassionTranslation.com.

Scripture quotations marked (AMP) are taken from the Amplified Bible, Copyright © 2015 by The Lockman Foundation. Used by permission.

Scripture quotations marked (ESV) are from The ESV® Bible (The Holy Bible, English Standard Version®), © 2001 by Crossway, a publishing ministry of Good News Publishers. Used by permission. All rights reserved.

Dedication

This book is my humble offering to God and to all the people who He knows by name that will be touched by the pages of this book. God, thank you for inviting me to partner in this work with you. This is all for your glory!

To those who believed this book would happen:

Your heartfelt prayers, fierce encouragement, and your depth of faith in God's call on my heart breathed this book to life. To each of you, I am eternally grateful. This is my gift to you.

Table of Contents

SECTION 1: RELEASE

SECTION 2: UNLEASH

SECTION 3: LAUNCH

Foreword

By Beth Johnson

The one where you're not a writer but one of the most wonderful friends God ever put in your path asks you to write her foreword...

When I tried to tell Megan I'm not a writer, she said something striking: "I always feel like you can tell when reading a foreword whether the person writing it actually knows the author and trusts their heart. I always look for forewords like that, because as a reader, you're opening yourself up to the spiritual insights of the author and that's really vulnerable. So, to have someone go first and let the reader know they are in good hands ... it matters."

So here I am, to let you know you're in good hands. I need more than a foreword to tell you about the trustworthiness of Megan's heart, but I'll refrain and just give a few examples. My kids (her mini-bffs) call her "fairy Godmother" and ask repeatedly when we will see her next. Her refrigerator is covered with their art and she has hosted them for Lego parties, art parties, pizza parties, and more. She is the ultimate gift giver, encourager, and listener. She gives the type of gift where the recipient tears up because they didn't even remember telling her how much they loved such and such. If sunsets and rainbows are your favorite, she searches for them and sends you pictures. Even during the hardest of times, Megan's heart is pointed toward her hope in God's goodness. She can find God in pizza rolls burning her tongue, rainy days, cloud formations, victories with her patients, and so much more. She has a "hope shelf" to remind her of the prayers that are not yet answered, but will be one day. Friends, one of the items on that shelf is a picture of a peanut butter sandwich. Want to know why? Because she believes God will heal my daughter's anaphylactic allergy. She has the kind of heart that believes for you even when you're not sure you still believe for yourself.

My friendship story with Megan began when she became my coworker at the end of 2015. I was admittedly sleep-deprived from having an infant and she was decidedly gracious and accepting. Our shared love for kiddos, especially those needing early intervention for autism, became evident quite quickly. The quality that ultimately connected us as not just co-workers, but friends, was curiosity. In the beginning, Megan was quietly curious, the kind of curious that acts like a sponge that dries quickly and immediately yearns for more. As I've come to know more of Megan, I've realized this is one of her most endearing qualities: the search for deeper meaning even in places where it is hard to find. Tenacious curiosity. Passion for not just accepting the bloom, but wondering what work it must've taken underground for the roots to produce such beauty.

And roots she has. Megan was in her mid-20's when she started asking if I could meet early before work for what we called "brain dumps." We pondered about life and have had so many questions for God along the way. We shared prayer requests and empathetic nods or hugs when we discussed the struggles with being soft-hearted empaths in a work environment that sometimes feels better suited for those of the leather-skin variety. Meg kept a list in her phone of questions she had for me or things that came up between meetings—we never once ran out of questions. When I had another infant and continued with my sleep-deprived pattern, she continued to give me grace on weeks I needed to cancel and was always there waiting, coffee and pen in hand, yearning for deep connection and understanding.

As I reflect back, these were really heart dumps, not brain dumps. They were the beginnings of stringing a deeper relationship with God and the foundation stones of a friendship. I also think many of the lines and connections drawn were the underpinnings of the blueprint for the book you're holding right now. We are reminded in Psalm 119 about storing God's Word in our heart. When we lay a foundation based on His Word and the murmurings of our hearts, beautiful things emerge.

You will find just that in the pages that follow: Megan's heart murmurings. But they aren't just random words that fell easily onto a page. The words here symbolize the countless hours she spent in quiet communion with her Father. They flow from the days she chose a 4:30am wake-up rather than snooze because God had called her into the darkness to prepare her roots for the book He wanted to bloom from her. (Let me pause here for a second, for those of you who don't know Megan. The girl loves sleep. She can fall asleep anywhere, anytime, despite being on her ninth cup of coffee–so when I say she has devoted countless hours before the sun comes up over the span of many years, searching God's Word, longing to know His heart in a more intimate way, and curiously connecting with others who are doing the same—that is no small feat.)

When a book is a branch from someone's heart, it hits different. When it's also a branch from God's heart, it's transformative. My prayer for you as you turn these pages is that you will allow Megan's words to soak into your soul. Spend no time hurrying to the next reflection, the next question, or even the next word until your heart says "go." Many eons ago, the prophet Isaiah was onto something that still applies to us today. It's no coincidence that people often leave off the end of this verse when quoted (italicized for effect): "Only in returning to me and resting in me will you be saved. In quietness and confidence is your strength. *But you would have none of it*" (Isaiah 30:15, NLT). The world we live in wants us to be list checker-offers. Don't make this book a to-do list item. Take it page by page, breath by breath, whether that takes you 30 days, 300 days, or 3 years. Let's be the ones who hear the first part of the verse and say "yes" to returning and resting in quietness and confidence. Let's be the ones who commit to taking time, pausing in God's presence, and dumping our hearts to Him.

A Note From the Author

This journal is the product of a journey God and I went on together. I felt a void when we were first quarantined to our homes in 2020. I found that by eliminating all my social engagements, my hour-long commutes to and from work, my weekly small group, and everything else I previously did outside my home, I faced a lot of free time and a choice of how to fill it.

In that time, God was drawing me closer. My curiosity to know more about Him was piqued. I decided to write down topics that I had genuine questions about. I wondered how to wait well, and how God sees me. I wondered about creativity and if that could actually be an avenue of connection with Him. I wanted to know what it could look like to have a thriving prayer life and how to tell the difference between happiness and joy. I spent months exploring these topics by looking up Bible verses and writing down all my questions, without filtering them. Then, once I was done, I spent about a few months going through the content like a daily devotional. I couldn't get enough. I felt like God was revealing new things to me in His Word and providing practical analogies to connect His Word to the world around me. That process genuinely changed my life. I learned that God not only welcomes our questions, but also loves to answer them. He delights in us discovering more of who He is and who we are because of Him.

What started as a pile of questions turned into an identity journey. What began as questioning a God who felt far away turned into a thriving personal relationship with our God, Emmanuel, who is with us. The following pages include fifty-two of those topics and many of my original questions. I imagine that maybe if I had these questions, others would, too.

The identity journey God took me on was both painful and beautiful. God started by helping me release the lies I believed, and then, in the spaces where those lies were once held, He unleashed His truth. As I write this, I'm standing at the brink of being fully launched into the abundant life God has for me. He has this abundant life waiting for you, too. The tangible transformation that occurred in me is indescribable. It's one thing to know the truth, but when it finally moves from your head to your heart, that's the moment we come alive. That is a holy moment.

As I moved through my own journey, asking God who He is and who I am through the context of the topics you are about to explore, God began shifting my heart towards writing, as if He was saying, "What I am doing in you, I want to do for others too. Share your story so others can see my heart for them." So here I am, following a call I never would have chosen for myself because I believe He has a message for YOU! This is my brave "yes."

It's time to bring our honest questions and deepest desires to Him. It's time to let Him displace lies we've believed and show us the truth. It's time for us to confidently embrace who we were created to be and walk through this life authentically, in the authority we have as children of God. YOU are a child of the King! To know what that means, we must dive more deeply into who God is and who He created you to be. We need to take these topics no longer at face value, but dive into the depths of it with Him. No longer will we sit and let His words bounce off of us without leaving an impression. Instead, we can choose this journal as a commitment to sit with His words, engage with them, and apply them. In 1 Corinthians 3:6-7 (NIV), Paul says, "I planted the seed, Apollos watered it, but God has been making it grow. So neither the one who plants nor the one who waters is anything, but only God, who makes things grow." God makes things grow, our faith included! While He is responsible for the growth, we also have a part to play. We get to cultivate the soil, water the seeds, and position ourselves where His light can reach us. He will do the rest.

So pour some coffee in your favorite mug and escape to a cozy spot with me. Let's invite God in and begin walking this journey together. It might be painful, it will definitely be beautiful, and it is absolutely worth it. Writing this book is my brave "yes," and maybe reading it is yours.

—Megan

SECTION 1

Release

This section of the book focuses on cultivating and stirring up the soil of our lives and releasing ourselves from anything that is tying us down so we are prepared to connect ourselves to the True Vine instead.

CHAPTER 1

Release

> *"Therefore, since we are surrounded by such a huge crowd of witnesses to the life of faith, let us strip off every weight that slows us down, especially the sin that so easily trips us up. And let us run with endurance the race God has set before us."*
> *-Hebrews 12:1 (NLT)*

My friend's daughter recently learned to walk. She held onto everything within arm's reach to help her stand. Whether it was a coffee table, a bookshelf, her mom's arm, or a wall, if it was close, she held on tight. Those were all solid and reliable things she could lean on as she figured out how to stand. The problem was she couldn't progress to walking until she was willing to let go. What was so good and necessary for her to learn one skill could no longer be a crutch. She had to release something good for something even better–the freedom to move around without assistance. It took courage from her and a lot of gentle coaxing and guidance from loving adults who were ready with arms wide open to catch her and cheer her on.

I imagine God is like that with us—standing in front of us, calling us to let go of the things that hold us back. He is ready to cheer us on and catch us if we fall, gently lifting us back to our feet.

So many daily challenges hold us back or trip us up. Burdens, difficulties, distractions, thought patterns, habits that aren't serving us … maybe we are over-scheduling commitments, under-scheduling rest, or are just in a season of life that feels heavy and overwhelming. Whatever the case, Hebrews 12:1 asks us to strip off and release every weight that slows us down so we can run the race God has set before us. This releasing process isn't always easy or fun. When God took me on a release journey, I released some things with joy and others with tears. I joyfully let go of unrealistic expectations and lies about how I'm not enough. I joyfully released my need to prove my worth and the exhausting people-pleasing habits that I had come to rely on to make my relationships feel secure. I'd love to say that my process of releasing looked like getting rid of all the bad stuff in my life, but in some cases, I also had to let go of some things that were good to make room for what was even better. During that process, I realized I had been gripping things tightly. With my hands closed, I was unable to receive anything new or better. So, through tears, I opened myself up to the possibility of a new job, the possibility of a new small group, and let God open me up to the ability to say no and to be more intentional with my "yes." At first it felt counter-intuitive, and sometimes even counter-cultural. Not everyone understood my decisions, myself included. But through persistent prayer and the practice of loosening my grasp, God planted hope within me that He had more for me than what I was experiencing.

As the end of one year approached and I started thinking about the year to come, I heard people asking God for a "word of the year." I had never done it before, but in talking with those who practiced this, they simply explained it as praying about what God might have in store for you in the next year and paying attention to recurring themes. So I decided to give it a try. When I asked Him to provide me with a word for the year, and the word "release" continued to resurface, I hoped it would be the year I released all the bad, heavy stuff, and that I would feel free. The good news is, I did feel more free! Unfortunately, though, the process included releasing things that were familiar and felt safe in exchange for the unknown abundance God promises. That was incredibly difficult, but in hindsight, I can see that it was precisely the catalyst for my growth. The choice to release those things made space for God to be released more fully in me and for me to be released more fully in this world. The releasing process God called me to led me to freedom like I've never known, and He's offering that to you, too.

How do we begin that process? First, we have to identify what is holding us back. Where are you playing it too safe? What are the things you're holding too tightly? Where are you feeling anxious or burdened? The next step is to pray about it! Ask God to confirm the issues you've identified and allow Him the space to reveal additional things you hadn't considered, trusting that He will guide you to more freedom.

Begin with small changes, and write down your thoughts and feelings as you go. Find supportive friends who can encourage and keep you accountable. Be patient with yourself! Allow yourself the grace to release what no longer serves you, making room for new and better things that God has in store. Remember—this race is a marathon, not a sprint. Every step forward is progress. Embrace the journey, allowing yourself to move from familiarity to freedom and from scarcity to abundance, knowing that God is with you every step of the way.

QUESTIONS TO CONSIDER:

1. What things are tripping you up or holding you back in life right now?

2. Is there anything God is asking you to release, let go of, or leave behind ?

   • What step can you take toward releasing one of those things?

3. Are there any good things God has been building inside you that He is asking you to release into the world, your neighborhood, community, or friend group?

   • What would it look like to say "yes" to God and release that thing to those people?

4. What could running with endurance, the race God has set before you, look like?

ACTIVITY:

BOXES

Label the boxes with things you are currently carrying that are holding you back from running your race. Envision yourself putting each box down, one by one. Imagine God in this scene. What would He be doing or saying as you're laying these boxes down?

CHAPTER 2

A Life of Prayer

*"At each and every sunrise you will hear my voice as
I prepare my sacrifice of prayer to you. Every morning I lay
out the pieces of my life on the altar and wait for your fire to
fall upon my heart."*
-Psalm 5:3 (TPT)

When we participate in prayer with God, we are opening ourselves up to the most powerful and enduring relationship we will ever have. So much overflows from our prayer lives, all due to the consistency and depth of our daily relationship with Him. Contrary to what I believed for most of my life, prayer can encompass much more than simply talking "at" God and there is no right way to do it. Prayer is a beautiful ebbing and flowing conversation where I talk *and* listen. It's also more than a conversation–it's a heart posture.

The New International Version of Psalm 5:3 says it this way, "In the morning, LORD, you hear my voice; in the morning I lay my requests before you and wait expectantly." Both this version and the one used at the beginning of this chapter use the word "wait." Wait, for what exactly? Personally, I think we are to wait not just for our prayers to be answered but for God to respond. It likely won't be audible, but leaving space for Him to respond allows thoughts and ideas to enter our minds and the fruit of His Spirit to flood our lives.

This is a reminder I constantly need. In 2023, I started a new rhythm of praying on my knees before bed each night. It was partially out of a desire to humble myself each evening in gratitude. Also, if I'm honest, I needed to change my posture for my evening prayers because otherwise, I'd be asleep mid-sentence.

The other night, I was praying on my knees. I went over the day and talked about what I was grateful for and ways I noticed God showing up, and then prayed over the things on my heart for the next day. Then I ended it like always: "I love you, Amen." And as I was standing up to get in bed, I felt this thought wash over me, as if He was whispering it straight to me: "Why don't you ever pause long enough for me to say it back?" It made me cry. Not because I felt ashamed or reprimanded in any way–I didn't. I was overwhelmed with love and with the realization that it matters to God that I know He loves me. Stopping to listen helps us to hear things like that.

If we want an intimate and personal relationship with God (He definitely does with us!), then communicating with Him is a significant avenue to fostering that relationship. Think about it in terms of friendship. If you spend your time learning about someone, talking about them, and reading about them, but not speaking to them, that doesn't amount to a relationship. That sounds a lot like my "relationship" with a few authors I admire. I read their books, listen to their podcasts, talk about them, and share the wisdom I've learned from them, but I've never spoken to them. They wouldn't know me if they passed me on the sidewalk. They aren't my friends.

Jesus though? He's my friend.

On the flip side, what a dull, one-sided relationship it would be if I never stopped to listen to what God had to say. He's not asking us to come to Him with our morning or nightly monologue. He's asking us to come, as we are, with all our thoughts and questions, concerns and excitements, and experience His comfort, peace, love, joy, compassion, grace, and so much more. Pausing to listen feels like opening my hands and preparing to receive whatever He has for me. Sometimes, that pause happens in my structured prayer time, but it also happens in the shower, driving to work, or walking through the neighborhood. There's no right or wrong time; it's just an opportunity to say I'm here, listening, and ready to receive. Sometimes, I hear him responding to these moments, not audibly, but through Scripture coming to mind or a thought that wasn't my own. Sometimes, I don't hear anything. In those moments when I feel His silence, I picture Him present with me, the same way a sweet friend would be after I vulnerably share my heart, lovingly looking back at me with eyes that say, "I'm here with you."

QUESTIONS TO CONSIDER:

1. What does prayer involve? And how is it a sacrifice?

2. What does it feel like/look like/sound like for you to "lay out the pieces of my life on the altar" and "wait expectantly"?

3. Do you struggle to bring any topics or areas of life to Him? If so, why do you think that is?

4. Consider your prayer life today. What is one thing you can do to build into your prayer life, approach it in a new way, or practice listening to His response?

ACTIVITY:

SCRIPTURE READ-ALOUD

Select a few verses of Scripture that resonate with you or hold personal significance.

Begin by reading the chosen verses. Enter a moment of prayer, seeking God's guidance on how the Scripture relates to your current life circumstances. Set a timer for 1 minute and pause to listen until the timer concludes.

Reread the verses aloud, then pause for a minute to reflect.

Explore a different translation of the Scripture and read it aloud in this new version. Take another minute to absorb the words.

Conclude the session with a heartfelt prayer, allowing a minute of silence before saying Amen.

If you hear something, feel something, have an emotional response, or a new insight, dedicate time to journaling about that experience.

If there's no immediate response, which is common, consider setting a reminder on your phone every two hours to pause briefly, affirm your willingness to listen to God, and attentively wait for any messages or insights He may share before returning to your routine.

CHAPTER 3

Known

"For you created my inmost being;
you knit me together in my mother's womb.
I praise you because I am fearfully and wonderfully made;
your works are wonderful,
I know that full well.
My frame was not hidden from you
when I was made in the secret place,
when I was woven together in the depths of the earth.
Your eyes saw my unformed body;
all the days ordained for me were written in your book
before one of them came to be.
How precious to me are your thoughts, God!
How vast is the sum of them!
Were I to count them,
they would outnumber the grains of sand—
when I awake, I am still with you."
- Psalm 139:13-18 (NIV)

A t times, I have struggled to believe that God knows me intimately. In moments of doubt and confusion, when life's path seems unclear and I cannot see how my present circumstances fit into a greater plan, I wonder if I am truly known and seen by Him. When my feelings feel too big, I wonder if He truly knows how I feel and can relate to someone who feels so deep and so wide. The vastness of the universe and the intricacies of life can feel overwhelming, and I question how an infinite God could be intricately involved in the details of my existence. Yet, these feelings of uncertainty are met with the reassuring words of Psalm 139:13-18, a reminder of God's deep and personal knowledge of me, a knowledge that transcends human understanding and affirms His intentional design and purpose for my life.

What I find most humbling about this passage is the reminder that every detail of who we are, whether we appreciate that detail or not, was purposeful. God can and will use all of it. He doesn't want to use us despite who we are or how we are, but because of it! If we can find the confidence that every detail of our creation was intentional, that we were intricately crafted, can't we also stand in the confidence that our present and future are equally as secure?

Jesus not only knows your name; He knows you completely. Everything about you is known to Him, thoroughly and intricately, for He created you. He understands your passions and what makes you laugh or cry. He knows the foods you like, the desires you have, and the gifts you bring to this world. He knows what hurts you and what heals you. He knows your mistakes and the decisions you've struggled with. He knows how you've failed or fallen, and He knows the ways you've gotten back up and tried again. He knows the color of your eyes and the things that light your soul on fire. He thinks you are marvelous! You *are* marvelous. Nothing you could do could make Him love you any more or any less. You are fully known *and* fully loved by God, right in this moment.

How can we act out of that confidence when doubts start creeping in? Something that helps me is to remember that God is active and present. I call on the Holy Spirit and speak truth out loud when the voices of doubt and uncertainty are deafening. I wrote out the following phrase to combat the doubts and repeated it as many times as necessary, until the truth became the loudest voice in the room: "You are the God of the details. My days are ordained and written in your book. Not just the number of my days, but the contents of them, too. My future is secure in You."

The more I say this simple phrase, the more it becomes ingrained within me. It settles me. Feel free to adopt this phrase or choose to write your own. As we speak truth over ourselves, it shifts something in our minds and our hearts. It may not make sense when I explain it in words, but it makes sense when I *feel* it. The Word is active and alive. As we say it and as we hear it, we set it loose to do its good work in us.

QUESTIONS TO CONSIDER:

1. How does it feel to be known so personally and intimately by God?

2. How do the verses above impact your view of yourself or God?

3. Knowing that God fully knows you can be so freeing because it means we can bring everything to Him. He already knows, but He loves to talk to us about it anyway! Is there anything you have been hesitant to bring to God? (Reminder: It doesn't just

have to be things we are ashamed of. It can be equally as scary to pour out our deepest desires to Him.)

4. What phrase can you repeat aloud when your doubts and uncertainty about your purpose and future become loud?

LETTERS

On the first piece of paper, write a letter to God. Welcome Him into some places you've been hesitant to let Him into. Then, on the second page, write His response. What would God say to you in response to your letter? Take time. Pause. Pray. And note whatever comes to mind.

Note: I know it can sometimes be a little uncomfortable to do an exercise like this if you've never thought about what God might say back to your prayers. Here are a few things I've found helpful:

1. Pay attention to your senses. What are you feeling? Internally? Externally?

2. Pay attention to any words, phrases, or ideas coming to you that weren't on your mind before.

3. Pay attention to any memories, Scripture passages, experiences, etc. that are brought to mind during this time.

4. Get curious about all of it and lean into the knowledge that God wants to speak to you.

5. If you're not sure if what you're hearing is truly God, that's okay! Discerning God's voice can be challenging! To help guide you in that, ask yourself, is this something Jesus would say? Does this align with Scripture? And then, if you're still

not sure, write it down and ask some friends who love you and love God and see if they think it sounds like something He would say to you.

6. Some reminders about who God is:

   - He is love

   - He is a guide

   - He is gentle

   - He corrects us, but does not shame us

   - He has good things for us

   - He wants us to experience more of Him and His heart for us

So if what you're hearing doesn't align with those characteristics, be willing to question it.

CHAPTER 4

He Calls You by Name

"The gatekeeper opens the gate for him, and the sheep recognize his voice and come to him. He calls his own sheep by name and leads them out. After he has gathered his own flock, he walks ahead of them, and they follow him because they know his voice."
- John 10:3-4 (NLT)

Jesus knows us. We are His own. He speaks to us *directly, personally*, by name—and we recognize His voice. There is something deeply profound about this truth. Jesus doesn't just issue a general invitation to follow Him—He calls each of us *by name*. It's intimate. It's relational.

Have you ever noticed how quickly you respond when someone says your name, even in a noisy room? Scientific research confirms that our brains respond in powerful, unique ways to hearing our name. Remarkably, even individuals in an unresponsive state often still record brain activity specifically when their names are being spoken. Coincidence? I think not. It's evidence of how we were wired from the beginning—created to respond to the One who calls us.

There's a part we play in this relationship, too. Jesus is always speaking, but we have to *tune in.* Like a radio host who's always broadcasting, His voice is constant. But it's up to us to turn the dial—through prayer, stillness, and reading His Word. He doesn't just call us once. He keeps speaking, leading, and guiding. The question is: *Are you listening?*

Interestingly, research studies show that we have a similar reaction in our brains when we hear our name as we do when engaging in activities and thoughts that are core to our identity. Our name is directly linked to our God-given identity. That means when Jesus calls us by name, He isn't just grabbing our attention—He's affirming our identity. When He says your name, He is speaking your God-given worth over you. He is calling you *daughter,* son, *beloved, chosen, known.*

But in our everyday lives, His voice isn't the only one we hear. There are other voices, too—some loud, some subtle—that try to define who we are. Maybe they come from people, your inner critic, or even the enemy. I've had to stop and ask myself: *What names am I hearing?* Is it "not enough"? "Too much"? "Unworthy"? Or is it "forgiven," "set apart," "mine"? When we filter those voices through the truth of who God is and how He speaks, it becomes clear which names come from Him—and which do not.

I remember one time on my way to work, I passed someone on the side of the road asking for food. I asked them if there was anything I could get them from McDonald's. They answered, and when I arrived at the drive-thru and was about to order, I felt like I had tuned in to God's voice. I had this feeling that wouldn't go away that I should get two meals instead of one. When I arrived back at the spot where the woman was standing, I noticed she was now with another person. I handed them the food, and they were so grateful, and I instantly realized that the God who knows *all* of our names was caring for each of us individually in that moment. He was showing me that I can be His hands and feet. And He was showing them that He meant it when He said He would supply all our needs.

This almost silly example is just one of many, where He chose to speak and I chose to respond. I invited Him in and He prompted me to do something. And the thing He prompted me to do mattered. There are other examples, too, where I unfortunately didn't answer. Maybe I was "too busy," or I wasn't sure it was really God. Since I didn't follow through, I'll never truly know. But the more that I learn His voice, and the more I trust and follow through on the things that sound like something He would do, the more confidence I gain in the sound of His voice. I believe wholeheartedly that when we step out in faith and do something in love, even if it wasn't directly prompted by Him, we are still becoming more like Him. Everything He does is done in love. So when we act in love, I believe it moves His heart.

He is calling you—with a heart full of love and longing for connection. He invites you into a journey far deeper than simply knowing you're His; it's a journey into the full understanding of your identity in Him and reaping the benefits of being His kid.

His voice becomes the compass of our faith—the foundation for making decisions, the source of our confidence, and the assurance that we are never alone. In recognizing His voice, we discover that we are seen, known, and called into something greater: a life anchored in His truth and shaped by His love.

So today, pause and listen. He is speaking your name. Are you tuned in?

Lord, help us to believe everything you say about us, no matter how beautiful.

QUESTIONS TO CONSIDER:

1. Recall a time you heard God's voice. How did you know it was Him? Are there any tools you use to differentiate His voice from your thoughts or another source?

2. How does it make you feel that God calls you specifically and by name?

3. List things you would consider core to your God-given identity. Why do you think God designed our brains in a way that would allow us to be reminded of those core things every time we hear our name?

4. Is there a characteristic on that list that you haven't nurtured in a while? How can you allow your soul to be filled so you can reclaim that characteristic again?

ACTIVITY:

NAMES

Write down all the words/names you've given yourself or that others have given you that you've been identifying with recently (good, bad, or ugly).

List some names God gives you and the words He uses to describe you.

Put a line through all the names you've called yourself or identified with that don't align with His truth.

Pick 3 of your "new names" and find corresponding Bible verses that illustrate that truth.

HELLO
my name is

HELLO
my name is

HELLO
my name is

HELLO
my name is
NEW

HELLO
my name is
NEW

HELLO
my name is
NEW

Bible Verse:

Bible Verse:

Bible Verse:

CHAPTER 5

Resting in God's Presence

"Where can I go from your Spirit?
Where can I flee from your presence?
If I go up to the heavens, you are there;
if I make my bed in the depths, you are there.
If I rise on the wings of the dawn,
if I settle on the far side of the sea,
even there your hand will guide me,
your right hand will hold me fast.
If I say, "Surely the darkness will hide me
and the light become night around me,"
even the darkness will not be dark to you;
the night will shine like the day,
for darkness is as light to you."
- Psalm 139:7-12 (NIV)

I used to overcomplicate the concept of being in the presence of God. I would go to great lengths to position myself in specific spaces, like a church or my designated quiet time chair, hoping to feel God's tangible presence. While I knew in my mind that God was always with me, I struggled to grasp the true meaning of His constant presence and how to discern it in the everyday moments of my life. It all felt too abstract, leading me to divide my life into two categories: the secular and the spiritual.

It required a shift in my perspective to allow me to recognize God's fingerprints on everything around me. Instead of always trying to create sacred moments, I began to look for the sacredness in my ordinary moments. When you genuinely have a relationship with Christ, the spiritual and secular boundary begins to blur. Ordinary moments can become spiritual, and God can meet you in the most unexpected places. When we break down this barrier, we realize there is nowhere we can go that is beyond His reach. Incorporating Psalm 139 into our daily walk with God means recognizing that He is intimately acquainted with our thoughts, actions, and desires. It challenges us to live our lives with a heightened awareness of His presence, not just in our quiet times of prayer and worship, but in every mundane task and interaction, too. After moving to a new city eight years ago, knowing only one person in a five hour radius, I became well acquainted with loneliness. It is something that unfortunately still plagues me during holidays when I can't be with my family, or when I've gone a long stretch without seeing friends. These verses remind me that I am never alone, and what I notice when I acknowledge that truth is that I stop seeking external momentary comforts and instead let the Comforter Himself begin to work. There is nowhere I can go where God isn't with me. Repeat that out loud for yourself. It's true for you, too!

God is omnipresent and cares about every aspect of our lives, which means He is just as present and active in our quiet time chair as He is in the drive-thru line and just as much in our workplace as He is in the mountains. When we acknowledge His constant companionship, we begin to seek His guidance, wisdom, and comfort throughout our day. We open our hearts to His leading and trust that He works in and through us in all circumstances. This awareness transforms our ordinary moments into opportunities for divine encounters, making our daily lives a beautiful journey in God's ever-present and loving presence.

I wonder what He's saying to us when we forget He's there. I wonder what He would say if we start to remember He's everywhere and choose to expect Him there.

Questions to Consider:

1. Think about a time when, beyond a shadow of a doubt, God made Himself known to you. How did He show up in that moment/experience?

2. When/where do you sense God's presence the most? Least?

3. Consider how He might show up for you in some of your daily tasks this week. How will you know it's Him?

4. What is one thing you can do to expect Him in an unexpected place today?

ACTIVITY:

DIGITAL DETOX

Practice presence. During activities this week, when you would typically be on your phone, watching TV, listening to music, or on a screen of some sort, intentionally choose to put it down. Say a quick prayer to invite God into whatever you're doing–cooking, cleaning, walking, driving to work, etc. Be present with God.

Later, on the tree below, write on the branches representing each activity from which you took a screen break. On the leaves, write down any thoughts, feelings, sensory experiences, etc., that emerged during those screen-free experiences. In the roots, write anything new that these experiences taught you about God, or any new ways you noticed His presence.

CHAPTER 6

Surrender

"When you live a life of abandoned love, surrendered before the awe of God, here's what you'll experience: Abundant life. Continual protection. And complete satisfaction!"
- Proverbs 19:23 (TPT)

Surrender is *active*, not *passive*. Abundant life, continual protection, and complete satisfaction are all things I want, but they come at a price—complete surrender. We have to decide if that's a price we are willing to pay.

A good friend of mine always talks about "for you, for me" gifts, which means they benefit both people. It could be a board game you'll play together, tickets to a show you'll see, or maybe something new for the home you share. Surrender is a "for you, for me" gift, too, and it comes straight from the giver of all good and perfect gifts! God loves when we surrender to Him; when we do that with our lives, desires, and the quest for control, it benefits us. Not only are those things in much more capable hands, but as Proverbs 19:23 shows, He blesses us with abundant life, continual protection, and complete satisfaction. All those things are available to us, but the key that unlocks them is in our hands. The key is surrender. It's like opening a treasure box; we won't truly know what is inside unless we are willing to take a risk. When we aren't living a surrendered life, we might thwart our ability to be fully satisfied right here and now. We strive, control, plan, and exhaust ourselves, trying to make things happen out of our own strength and timing. If we make decisions that contradict where God is leading, it's not that He can't protect us there, but it's easy to see how the path He is paving for us is already paved with protection. There is security within His will.

There are countless desires I have that, as of now, are unmet. There are countless situations I try to control or fast forward through or where I desperately crave answers on why, when, and how...

Most of the time, I don't get the answers I'm looking for. My mind craves understanding. I want to know specific timelines on when my prayers will be answered, I want explanations when things don't happen the way I thought they would, and when facing a decision, I want the whole plan laid out for me step by step like an instruction manual. Instead, when I ask God why, when, and how, He often responds with a question: "Will you trust me?"

What depth of faith arises when we trust the One who loves us and works all things together for our good before the questions are answered? Can we trust God with our unmet desires, questions, and confusion, and surrender it all to Him? He knows, much more than we do, that what we actually need is not more information, but a deeper reliance on the One who knows all. We may never have abundant material things, money, friendships, or success. I don't believe that's what God promises us here. The promise we can hold onto is that when we surrender to God, He redefines abundance for us. We can find abundant life and joy even amidst the most challenging circumstances because our abundance is found in Him.

QUESTIONS TO CONSIDER:

1. Why is surrender essential?

2. Why do you think abandoned love and surrender are prerequisites to abundant life, continual protection, and complete satisfaction?

3. What is something you need to surrender?

4. Why is it hard to surrender what you named in the previous question?

ACTIVITY:

ROCKS AND CHAINS

Write what you want to surrender on the chains and rocks pictured below. Recognize that each holds weight; as you leave them there, you can leave lighter and freer than before. Pray over each of these things, and remember, when you truly surrender and cast your cares upon the Lord, leave them there, for He cares about you. Until you can empty your hands of the weights you carry, you will not have open hands to receive the things He has for you.

CHAPTER 7

Breaking Strongholds

*"For though we live in the world, we do not wage war as the
world does. The weapons we fight with are not the weapons of
the world. On the contrary, they have divine power to demolish
strongholds. We demolish arguments and every pretension that
sets itself up against the knowledge of God, and we take captive
every thought to make it obedient to Christ."*
- 2 Corinthians 10:3-5 (NIV)

Miriam-Webster Dictionary defines a stronghold as a structure or place from which one can resist attack. The word "stronghold" is listed in the Bible approximately fifty times and is discussed in two significant ways. The first way refers to things that keep us in bondage and hold us back from God, which occurs in 2 Corinthians 10:3-5. The second way it's referenced is God Himself being our stronghold, as in Psalm 27:12 (NIV) where David writes, "The Lord is the stronghold of my life." When I imagine a stronghold, I picture giant, immovable stone walls with a moat and drawbridge, and I'm inside. The thing about a fortress like that is that not only does it keep things out, but it also holds things in. In my own life, I know there have been times when the walls in my life were keeping God out and keeping lies inside. But here's the gift He gives us—we have the power to tear down those strongholds. I realized that since these strongholds are spiritual, it requires spiritual weapons to tear them down. And while it may feel exhausting to tackle these head-on, God offers Himself to replace the walls we think are protecting us. When we let God in to help us demolish the things keeping us from Him, He becomes the One surrounding us, protecting us and deciding what stays and what needs to go.

I confess that I often find myself seeking shelter in old stories, lies, and old versions of myself because, even though they aren't good places for my mind to settle into, they are familiar. Being out in uncharted territory is sometimes more challenging and scarier than staying in familiarity. As I reflected on this pattern within myself, I was reminded that there are statistics listing high percentages of individuals who have been previously incarcerated to re-offend, getting themselves landed back in jail. The research shows that the prison system provides predictability, familiarity, and safety, and often, it feels more comfortable to stay in that environment than to try to navigate the uncertainty of the world outside those prison walls. Even though it results in losing their freedom, that percentage of people choose familiarity over freedom.

Aren't there ways we each choose that in our lives, too? Familiarity has more of a hold on us than we think. It is a cunning thief, but no longer. Jesus has set us free, and the only thing He wants us to be bound by is Himself. May we boldly step into the uncharted, trusting in Jesus to be our ultimate anchor rather than clinging to the false security of the familiar.

QUESTIONS TO CONSIDER:

1. What are some of the strongholds you feel in your life right now? Write them down, and under each one, list how you think they have power over you.

2. What spiritual weapons do you have access to, and how can you use them to demolish strongholds? (Think about worship, prayer, scripture, vulnerability, friendships, and the ways you can participate in those things intentionally when it comes to strongholds.)

3. The word for stronghold in Greek is "oxýrōma." This word, described in the *Strong's Exhaustive Concordance of the Bible*, is defined as "a heavily fortified containment of a false argument in which a person seeks shelter to escape reality."[1]

   Think about this–what strongholds might you be seeking shelter in? Are your strongholds holding you, or are you holding onto them?

4. What is one practical step you can take to begin releasing the negative strongholds in your life?

---

1 James Strong, *Strong's Expanded Exhaustive Concordance of the Bible* (Nashville: Thomas Nelson, 2009), 3794.

ACTIVITY:

FORTIFIED WALLS

Picture your life with those fortified walls around it. What are the things you'd want to be kept in, what needs to go, and what would you like to be protected from? Write and draw it out in the illustration below.

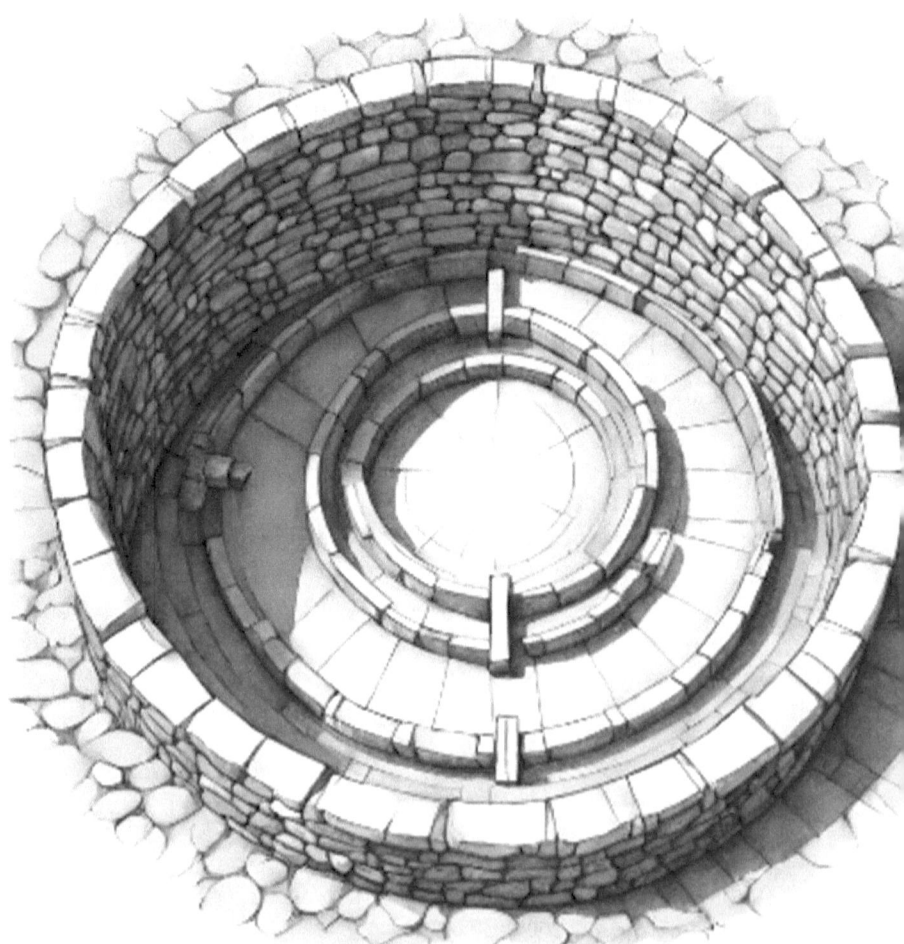

CHAPTER 8

Renewing Your Mind

"Do not conform to the pattern of this world, but be transformed by the renewing of your mind. Then you will be able to test and approve what God's will is—his good, pleasing and perfect will."
- Romans 12:2 (NIV)

One of my favorite things to do is watch the sunrise. Every morning, when I'm pouring my coffee, I look out the window in anticipation of seeing the gorgeous swirl of colors that God brushes across the sky. The one thing that bothers me is a dirty window. You can't truly see the beauty of His creation through a window with smudges obstructing your view.

Just as the radiance of the morning sun is dimmed by the smudges on a window, our perception of God can likewise be clouded by the blemishes of this world. What acts as a smudge in your life might be different than mine, but we all face internal and external struggles and pressures that have the capability to obstruct our view. Our hearts yearn for the unfiltered beauty of who He is and an un-inhibited connection with Him. Yet, these smudges, the residual impact of some of our earthly experiences, cloud our vision of God and our understanding of who we are in Him.

A few years ago, I found myself wondering what smudges existed in my life. I had to find out for myself using what seemed like a silly little activity. In my journal, I drew two windows next to each other and put "smudges" all over them. On the smudges, I wrote things in my life that prevent me from seeing the world and God's kingdom clearly. I had a pretty extensive list: my desire for things other people have (a house, a husband, and kids), comparison, fear, life circumstances, pressure to do things on a specific timeline, my tendency to neglect my own needs, etc. I studied this list for a while, wondering how to remove these smudges from my life. As someone who loves a good "to-do" list, I was excited. I figured, well, I'll just come up with a list of ways to "clean" or combat each smudge. I'll cross each one off the list, and I'll be seeing clearly by the end of the week. What I realized surprised me. Every task I listed on my "to-do" list fell into one of two categories: the need to stand more firmly on who God says He is or the need to rest more completely in the knowledge of who I am in Him. When I sat with that information, something became clear to me. These smudges revealed that I couldn't truly know who I was created to be if I didn't know my Creator, and I couldn't know the fullness of His character if I didn't know myself.

The renewal process, as discussed in Romans 12:2, is not merely an act of cleaning the surface; it is a profound, transformative change, akin to replacing the old window with a new one. This new window is clearer, stronger, and more resilient, crafted through our growing relationship with God. It involves shedding the old narratives we tell ourselves and embracing the truth in His Word.

Renewing our minds is a daily choice and a daily pursuit. It involves consciously filling ourselves with God's truth and aligning our thoughts daily. This means praying, reflecting on Scripture, being part of the Body of Christ, and being still in His presence. In these moments of quiet communion, we begin to discern God's will–His good, pleasing, and perfect will for our lives.

Even after all the work I've done on my identity, some areas of my life still feel shaky. I've taken the time to sit with and explore the moments when my heart and mind quickly travel a well-worn path that isn't serving me anymore ... moments when I know the truth, but my mind is so used to trailing away with an old story that before I know it, I'm right back down the rabbit hole. I created these old pathways, time after time, believing these lies were true, and while they still exist, I'm choosing to travel a different way. A way that can only be traveled with God leading the way.

As we continue this journey of renewal, let us strive to see the world not as a place of smudges and imperfections, but through the lens of God's transformative love. With each sunrise, let us be reminded of the new beginnings and endless possibilities that come with a mind renewed in Christ. Through this renewed mind, we can truly embrace the beauty of His creation, understand our purpose in His kingdom, and walk confidently in the identity He has given us.

QUESTIONS TO CONSIDER:

1. What are the specific "smudges" on your window that distort your view of God's plan for your life? How do they affect your daily decisions and feelings?

2. What experiences or beliefs have led to these "smudges"? Are they rooted in past events, societal pressures, or internal fears? Something else?

3. In what ways has comparing your life journey to others' created smudges on your window? How can you shift your focus from comparison to contentment in God's unique plan for you?

4. How can regular engagement with Scripture help in cleaning these smudges? Are there specific verses or Biblical stories that speak to your situation?

ACTIVITY:

Engage with the illustration of the window and smudges below to visually represent what you're reflecting on. Name the smudges, identify ways to engage with God's truth in order to clean those smudges, and consider what you might see once God's truth has clarified your view.

CHAPTER 9

Armor of God

"Therefore, put on every piece of God's armor so you will be able to resist the enemy in the time of evil. Then after the battle you will still be standing firm. Stand your ground, putting on the belt of truth and the body armor of God's righteousness. For shoes, put on the peace that comes from the Good News so that you will be fully prepared. In addition to all of these, hold up the shield of faith to stop the fiery arrows of the devil. Put on salvation as your helmet, and take the sword of the Spirit, which is the word of God. Pray in the Spirit at all times and on every occasion. Stay alert and be persistent in your prayers for all believers everywhere."
- Ephesians 6: 13-18 (NLT)

Before I go outside each day, I have to get dressed. The attire might change depending on the weather, but the routine remains consistent—shirt, pants, socks, shoes. It's a daily repetition. When kids first learn to dress themselves, they navigate the intricacies of armholes, head placement, and which foot goes into which shoe. Mistakes are inevitable, occasionally getting things backwards or inside-out. Eventually, they get the hang of it. It can be challenging to remember as adults, but we were once amateurs, too. The more we practiced, the more natural it became, and now, I'd bet you probably put your shoes on the right feet without a second thought. The analogy to our spiritual armor is strikingly similar. We have a designated set of armor to put on every single day. The more we practice, the more natural it becomes. We may have to think very intentionally about each item we put on at first, but as we consistently follow God's guidance, the process becomes smoother. The armor begins to feel increasingly familiar and comfortable. That familiarity is critical. If we limit putting on this armor to just our spiritual battles, it's no different than sliding into those special occasion shoes—uncomfortable and blister-inducing. We can't just sporadically throw on our armor, treating it like some stiff pair of shoes. When the battles arise, we'll really want well-worn, time-tested clothes, but there's only one way to break in our armor- we have to wear it daily.

What always strikes me as I read Ephesians 6 is that the armor we are asked to put on is the armor of God. Sit with that for a minute.

It's God's own armor.

He knows exactly what we're fighting against and what we need for protection, and He is offering it to us, tailored specifically for each of us and our needs. He knows our strengths and where our weak points are, and He's got us covered–literally! Our job is to put it all on. But how?

- We gain His truths through engaging regularly in Scripture and praying in alignment with those truths. The enemy loves to attack us through lies. If the truth is firmly rooted within us, we can deflect anything that tries to come against it.

- We practice wearing the breastplate of righteousness by acting on those truths as we go about our day. It's our choice to be full of integrity and authenticity.

- The shoes of peace steady us, and we find that peace by following God's lead in our lives. Peace and comfort are not synonymous. We may have to do the uncomfortable thing when we follow Jesus, but His peace surpasses our understanding.

- Our relationship with the Lord holds up the shield of faith. His faithfulness to us and His promises restore and rejuvenate our faith, enabling us to withstand any doubt, anxiety, or spiritual attack that comes against us.

- The helmet of salvation protects our minds. With our salvation in mind, we get to operate out of a place of hope and the knowledge that Jesus already won the battle for us—this battle, the next one, and every other battle forever.

- The last piece of armor is the sword of the Spirit, which is the Word of God. It's our only offensive equipment. Everything else is meant to defend, but the sword is meant for attack. I love that our mechanism for attack does not come out of our strength, but from the words God has already given us.

So, it's not just about putting on clothes; it's about wrapping yourself in the strength, truth, and peace that God provides. Each piece plays a vital role in facing the challenges of your day with a heavenly confidence. We are not ill-prepared for battle. It is, however, by an every day familiarity with our heavenly armor that it begins to make a difference.

Let this be our rally cry: to put on the armor of God not out of fear, but out of faith; not out of duty, but out of devotion. Let us be intentional in our preparation, mindful of the spiritual warfare that surrounds us. And as we journey forward, may the armor of God be our constant reminder of His unfailing love, His unshakeable truth, and His ultimate victory. We have all that we need. Time to suit up!

QUESTIONS TO CONSIDER:

1. How does it make you feel knowing that an unseen battle of darkness is happening in your life?

2. Which pieces of armor are most effortless for you to put on? Hardest?

3. Take some time to journal about the different pieces of armor and the clothing items/materials they are associated with. What parallels is God revealing to you about how we use those pieces of clothing for our physical body compared to what that piece of armor does for our mind and spirit?

4. What do you think it would look like/feel like for you to put on the WHOLE armor of God?

Activity:

SELF-PORTRAIT WITH A TWIST

Draw a self-portrait—incorporate the elements of the armor of God into your image. Showcase how these spiritual qualities are integral to your identity and daily life.

Draw any images that come to mind and jot down any words you think of.

CHAPTER 10

Words have Power

> *"The tongue has the power of life and death,*
> *and those who love it will eat its fruit."*
> *- Proverbs 18:21 (NIV)*

For most of my life, I underestimated the power of my words, specifically in how I spoke about myself. I let self-deprecating speech and lies repeatedly play in my head and out of my mouth until I lost the ability to untangle it all. I recognized that how I talked about myself directly impacted my beliefs and behaviors. I had to change the way I spoke first, and when I did, everything else changed too.

I used to call myself anxious because, occasionally, I would have seasons of anxiety. I didn't know it then, but those seasons didn't define me. By continuously calling myself anxious, I began to believe I *was* anxious. It gave me a cop-out for any new experience I was a little scared to try and gave fuel to my discomfort. I also called my-self too sensitive, and by believing that lie, I hid my emotions from others for fear of being too much for them, squashing my ability to cultivate authentic relationships. The thing about these defining words is that the more we speak them over ourselves, the more deep-ly ingrained they become and the more difficult it is to detach our-selves from them. A great example of that is how I had weight issues as a kid and was labeled ugly and fat. To compensate, I wore baggy clothes and hoodies year-round. I've since become much healthier, and I'm honestly happier with my body, but that lie is still subcon-sciously ingrained. I notice that no matter the weather, I'm likely wearing a hoodie. It's not even about the lie anymore–God has re-deemed all of that. But because I believed them for so long, hoodies have become what I feel most comfortable in. It's hard to part with items or habits that have acted as a crutch through difficulty. But I'm not shaming myself for that. I first have to acknowledge it, and then I get the opportunity to make a conscious choice. I can appre-ciate my God-given body for the ways it can move, for the strength it has, and for the gifts it offers to me and others. These habits that we create to compensate for the lies we believe about ourselves run deeper than we think, but we don't have to stay stuck there, and we don't have to speak those lies over ourselves anymore.

Words have much power, and that power isn't confined to our own lives. There are countless Biblical examples where we are told to encourage one another and love one another well. In my own expe-riences, the first people to speak life to my dreams and truth against lies were the people who loved me. When I couldn't see the lie for myself, or when my language continued to reflect an old narrative, other people stepped in, and I'm grateful they did!

One of the most profound examples of this happened within the last few years. I deeply desire to be married and have a family of my own, and I used to joke about being single forever or being the eternal third wheel. Hiding behind jokes helped numb the fear that my desires would never be fulfilled. I never admitted out loud or even in writing that that's what I wanted because what if it didn't happen, or God didn't do it? What if I let myself hope, and my hope was crushed? But despite my best effort to keep those desires locked up inside of me, a few close friends, in the most beautiful way, instinctively knew how I felt. I didn't have to say it out loud for them to see it in my eyes or recognize it in my spirit. It's how God created me. At age fifteen, I was affectionately labeled the mom of a mission trip, and I couldn't think of a higher compliment. My loving and nurturing spirit was not a last-minute ingredient when He created me. Instead, it is deeply ingrained in the fabric of my character.

As friends began to notice that hidden desire inside me, I noticed that their language shifted. They'd say things like "when you get married" or "when you have kids." They started speaking life to something that I, for so long, was too scared to let myself hope for. There was expectation in their voice and hope in their hearts. Even my friend's sweet five-year-old told me she couldn't wait for me to have kids so she could play with them. I can't help but recognize how she emulated her mom's language at that moment and spoke just as much life into my dreams as any faith-filled adult. As each of them began to speak in faith and expectation, the way I started to speak and pray drastically changed too.

Maybe you have labeled yourself "anxious." Perhaps you're struggling to let yourself believe your illness will be healed. Maybe you still remember that teacher who called your question dumb or that uncle who made fun of how much you ate at Thanksgiving dinner. Maybe you think about the names your unkind junior high peers called you or the ways your parents described you growing up. Maybe you still believe those things. Or maybe it's a long-buried dream you still have, and you're unsure you have what it takes to publish that book, open that business, pursue a new career, or step into the ministry God has called you to. Whatever it is, there is encouragement, life, and goodness that need to be spoken, and some lies need to be silenced too. Today is the day.

I am confident that my life is wildly different because of the life that has been spoken into me, the lies that no longer have a voice, and the prayers that have been offered up on my behalf. My voice matters in my life and in the lives of others, and yours does too.

QUESTIONS TO CONSIDER:

1. What are some of the words you most commonly speak over yourself? Out of those, identify which ones you believe are truth and which are lies.

2. What are some things that you are currently speaking death to that need to live or speaking life to that need to die?

3. What are some practical ways you can begin speaking to yourself, your dreams, desires, future, identity, etc., in ways that bring life?

4. How can you use your voice to speak into your friends' lives? Be a noticer and keep your ears open for opportunities to do that this week. On this side of Heaven, we may never know the true impact of our encouragement and the result of our heart-

felt prayers. But know that it matters, and every single time you pause to do that, the Lord is with you.

ACTIVITY:

Fill out the following table. Consider both broader areas of your life ("identity" or "career," for example) and very specific things like that one particular lie that keeps playing in your head or that one fear that is holding you back

Areas of my life that need LIFE spoken to them	Areas of my life that need DEATH spoken to them

*if you are struggling to distinguish if something is a lie, praying about it, looking in God's Word, and confiding in a close, trusted friend are great ways to start.

CHAPTER 11

The God who fills me

"For He satisfies the thirsty and fills the hungry with good things."
- Psalm 107:9 (NLT)

One of my favorite things about God is that He promises to fill us. I can't tell you how many times I've felt like I was lacking something–community, joy, money, energy, focus, answers to my prayers, vision, purpose, the fulfillment of my deepest desires... or sometimes, like a recipe I thought I followed to a T, I can't quite put my finger on what's missing. Still, the end product tasted a little off.

God promises to be our provider. Psalm 23 says that because the Lord is our Shepherd, we have all we need. Jesus even calls Himself the Bread of Life–the bread that sustains us. So why do we sometimes feel these gaps between what we have and what we feel we need? It's easy to let our thoughts be consumed with all the lack. But we no longer need to operate from a scarcity mindset. Our Father is the God of abundance!

With this new perspective, I've allowed these moments in my own life to become opportunities to shift my focus from the gap to the gap filler. Often, it's not that there is a gap He didn't fill; I just had my mind set on how I wanted Him to fill that gap, and He filled it differently. One major example of this was my search for a house. Years ago, I very clearly felt God calling me to put down roots. I believed He wanted to fill my gap for a place of my own and my lack of belonging to a community through a house in a neighborhood. What ended up happening was quite different. Not only did I end up unexpectedly moving out of a place I shared with friends in Northern Kentucky and moving across the state line into Cincinnati, I also moved into a smaller apartment than the one I had previously. My eyes were so fixed on believing a house was the way He was going to fill that gap that I completely missed the blessing at first. The small apartment I moved into was right down the street from my friend and her family. That proximity was the catalyst for a level of belonging I never even knew to pray for. It consisted of opportunities to pick up things from the store for each other, spend time sipping early morning coffee on the porch, lunchtime walks, after work chats, time spent playing with the kids, surprise treats and flowers left on the porch on birthdays and hard days, and so much more. It also allowed me two years of saving money for the house that I would eventually buy. What I thought was a setback was actually an answer to my prayer and the catalyst for my ultimate dream of a home in a neighborhood. When my eyes and prayers are so focused on the avenue through which I want to be filled, I tend to miss what He is really doing. I don't want to miss it anymore. There are many places in our lives and hearts that the world has conditioned us to try to fill with worldly things. I've struggled with that, too, especially when I feel like He isn't providing. It's easy to take things into my own hands and then try to regain control and fill myself. Those things will never measure up. They will always be a counterfeit for the filling God provides. I'm not saying He won't provide with worldly things; He does that, too! But first and foremost, He fills the gaps with Himself.

Need vision for your life? The only one who can provide that is the One who has predestined good works for you. Need fulfillment of your deepest desires? The more time you spend with the Lord, the more your desires align with His, and the more He becomes your deepest desire. Need money? If you're anything like me, He might ask you to trust Him with what you have first. (Ooof, I know.) But learning to rely on Him and trust Him to come through are beautiful lessons that deeply matter. Because in the process of learning those lessons, we are building a history with God that we will someday look back on and say, "I can trust Him now because He was faithful then." Whatever you feel like you need, bring it to Him and recognize that an answered prayer may not be in the form of the thing you're asking for, but God himself.

QUESTIONS TO CONSIDER:

1. Where are the gaps between what you have and what you feel you need?

2. Look up the Biblical definitions for "satisfies" and "fills" and write about what you're noticing about what God is promising to do for you here.

3. Think of how God has satisfied and filled you in the past. Has it always happened the way you thought it would? How does that impact your posture as you approach your current needs?

4. What is one thing you can do today to allow yourself to receive the filling God has for you?

ACTIVITY:

BUCKETS

You can pour into a bucket all day, but if there is a hole in the bottom, it will never truly be filled. Before you can be filled in those areas above, can you identify any leaks in your life? Are there any areas where you are being drained? Use the illustration below to reflect on what areas you find yourself drained of and what God might want to do to patch those holes so He can fill you to overflowing.

CHAPTER 12

El-Roi -The God Who Sees

> *"But whenever you pray, go into your innermost chamber and be alone with Father God, praying to him in secret. And your Father, who sees all you do, will reward you openly."*
> *- Matthew 6:6 (TPT)*

Somewhere within us, there is still that longing for Eden ... to be seen, known, and loved in the way we were created to be. After Adam and Eve ate the fruit, they covered themselves and hid, which means that before that moment, they were fully seen and fully known by God, completely unashamed. Yet God's perception of them remained steadfast, unaffected by their attempt to conceal themselves. He didn't see them any less because they were hiding. He didn't know them any less because they were filled with shame. We still experience a longing for that uninhibited, intimate connection with God. It's ingrained in us, whether we are consciously aware of it or not. That level of connection is still available to us, and we can find it by directing our yearning towards the Lord. When you feel that yearning, try asking, "Who am I seeking recognition from?" I think what we find is that our true longing isn't of this world. It's something much more profound.

In the quiet moments of prayer, we are reminded that our Father is El-Roi, the God Who Sees. It's a truth that resonates in the very fabric of our existence. In a world where visibility and recognition often shape our pursuits, we find solace in the knowledge that God sees us intimately, beyond the external façade we may present. With Him, we can exhale, let our walls down, and just be. The verse above from Matthew 6:6 urges us to retreat into the innermost chamber of our hearts, to be alone with Father. It is in this sacred space that we can lay bare our desires to be seen, known, and loved. We recognize that regardless of what others see or don't see, God's gaze remains unwavering. In the rhythm of daily life, where our efforts may go unnoticed by the world, God's recognition becomes the ultimate affirmation. Our daily endeavors matter to Him, and His blessings are poured out consistently, not just in some distant heavenly future. Let's open our eyes to these daily blessings, recognizing that each act of love, every moment of integrity, and every choice for grace is acknowledged by the God Who Sees.

As we navigate this journey, doing the mundane day after day, let's be mindful of our motives. Seek recognition, not from the world, but from the One who intimately knows the depths of our hearts. Let His approval be the one we seek. Someday, when God utters those words, "Well done, good and faithful servant," it won't be a checklist of grand gestures. It'll be a resounding affirmation for every small act of kindness and every expression of love ... every dish you washed, every lunch you packed, every encouraging text you sent, every time you said "yes" to God in obedience when those around you didn't agree, every time you stood at the cash register with a friend and said, "I've got it, it's my treat"... A compilation of moments like this makes for a life well lived. So, take a moment to slow down, lay yourself open at His feet, and hear His whispered words, "Well done, well done, well done."

QUESTIONS TO CONSIDER:

1. Are there things that you wish people saw or appreciated more often? List them.
   - How does it feel to know God sees these things?

2. What rewards/blessings are you seeing in your life?
   - Consider blessings that aren't visible to the eye- a shift in perspective, a molding of your character, or maybe a depth to the way you display the fruits of the spirit.

3. What do the things you do in secret say about your:
   - Character
   - Identity
   - Relationship with God

4. If you could hear God tell you He is proud of you for one thing right now, what would you most want to hear Him say?

ACTIVITY:

GLASSES

In the first pair of glasses, write or illustrate the achievements or successes that the world (and the people in your life) commonly recognize. What accomplishments or milestones do you think society values?

In the second pair of glasses, write or illustrate what you think God sees, recognizes, and values. Reflect on the difference between these two illustrations. Think about one practical way this week you can choose to put on God's lens instead of the world's.

CHAPTER 13

My Comforter

"Whenever my busy thoughts were out of control,
the soothing comfort of your presence
calmed me down and overwhelmed me with delight."
- Psalm 94:19 (TPT)

I love comfort. My home is full of soft pillows, fleece blankets, an electric fireplace, a bean bag chair, and I have a sectional that feels about as close as you can get to sitting on a cloud. Beyond physical comforts, I also crave emotional and mental comfort. Sometimes that has looked like avoiding situations that I thought would make me uncomfortable–social engagements, trying new activities, hard conversations, speaking up, setting a boundary, or doing things by myself or for myself. I'm historically not one to choose anything out of my comfort zone. Nine times out of ten, I will choose comfort over just about anything. I learned a few years ago, though, that maybe the goal in life isn't for us to be comfortable, and perhaps the comfort I was seeking was counterfeit.

One of the scariest things God called me to do was to start sharing my writing with others. It was only a few years ago that I began journaling for myself. Those writings felt more vulnerable than anything I've ever done. My honest questioning, my curiosity, my most gut-wrenching prayers, and my most heartfelt desires were all there in blue ink. Page after page, I filled up countless journals. I started with a gentle "yes," and slowly, it was as if God was saying, "Will you come out a little deeper?" "Can you trust me with more?" What started as me sharing tidbits of my heart through words in social media captions has since turned into an entirely writing-dedicated account, countless articles published, and the inception of this book. I'd love to say the growth between points A and B was linear, but it wasn't. It was full of questions and doubts, but those were the exact things that pulled me closer to the One with the answers. I talked to Him about so much! It's easy to feel like we don't need that constant conversation with the Lord when things are comfortable. The uncertainty I felt around my circumstances was the avenue through which His invitation to "come to me" was finally received and accepted in full.I remember walking into a small group many years ago and saying God was leading me out of my comfort zone. I had no idea what that might mean and could never have guessed the journey following that call would entail. All I knew was that God was inviting me into new spaces with Him, and I had a choice to make. I could say "yes" or I could say "no". "No" was tempting, but I couldn't shake the feeling that God had something more for me, something that my craving for comfort was isolating me from. Stepping out of my comfort zone meant trusting God in a new way.

It felt like jumping off a cliff and wondering if He'd catch me. It started with moments like volunteering to pray out loud, attending group yoga classes, and beginning to share myself vulnerably with others. As I practiced those things, God started calling me to step out into deeper levels of uncertainty. Through a culmination of many smaller yeses, I built my trust in Him. What I've always loved about my comfort zone is that it makes me feel secure. That security was a knockoff of the comfort only God can provide. God offered to be my true security even when everything else felt uncertain around me. What I really needed was Him! In uncertainty, my mind tends to race. Busy thoughts? Yep. A million questions? Yep. Overwhelmed by all the scenarios? Yep. I get worked up, and I feel a wide spectrum of emotions. The list goes on and on. But our good God promises us something in these moments, and the promises, like this one in Psalm 94:19, bring me comfort too. Busy thoughts? Soothed. Overwhelmed with circumstances? He'll overwhelm you with delight. Worked up? He'll calm you down. Wherever you feel uncomfortable, He is there, and His presence is enough.

Since starting my writing journey, it has been abundantly clear that all of my growth has happened in moments when I didn't feel comfortable. My confidence was built. My faith was strengthened. Active endurance became such a lifestyle that I got it tattooed on my arm. I always wanted to grow, to be more me and more whole. But growth can't occur without stretching or newness, without delays and pauses, mountains and valleys, questions and answers, and a balance of familiarity and discovery. If everything remained the same, I would never learn anything new about myself or about Him, and I could easily be tricked into thinking I was just fine without Him. If the boat is never rocked, I'll never know if I was truly built to sail.

God met me in the middle of all those uncomfortable moments and comforted me far beyond what a fleece blanket or a cozy sectional ever could. God showing up for me right in the middle was more than enough.

Because our God is one of abundance, His comfort encompasses more than just His presence. He actually wired us with built-in tools we can use for comfort, like our breath, our ability for intentional movement, and how we feel after a good hug or a good cry. I don't think God is as concerned with the same types of comforts I used to be. When God leads me into uncomfortable situations (and He often does), He wants to be the One that comforts us. His comfort doesn't look like escaping the situation but walking with us through it and helping us utilize those tools we are wired with. It's not that God wants us to be uncomfortable. But He *does* want us to grow, and He knows something that took me a long time to learn: growth happens outside our comfort zones.

QUESTIONS TO CONSIDER:

1. Reflect on times when God has comforted you in the past. How does God typically express His comfort to you?

2. Are there any places in your life where you avoid uncomfortable circumstances/interactions to preserve your comfort? If so, what is God saying to you about those things and the kind of growth He has for you there?

3. As you think about those uncomfortable situations, is there anything you are seeking for comfort in those areas besides Him?

4. Where is God inviting you to step out of your comfort zone with Him?

ACTIVITY:

Take a moment to explore the reason that staying in your comfort zone is so enticing. Imagine your comfort zone as a space that feels protected, where you're surrounded by the things that bring you a sense of control and peace. What is it isolating you from? The possibility of pain? The opportunity for joy? Something else? What is your comfort zone allowing you to control or protect?

What growth do you believe is possible for you on the other side of your comfort zone?

What do you think you'll need to walk through between point A (your comfort zone) and point B (the growth you seek)?

Write and draw it out in the illustration below. Let the chair signify your comfort zone and the mountain signify the growth available outside your comfort zone.

CHAPTER 14

Falling in Love with the You God Made

"For we are God's handiwork, created in Christ Jesus to do good works, which God prepared in advance for us to do."
- Ephesians 2:10 (NIV)

Have you ever paused to consider the profound truth that you are God's handiwork? In a world obsessed with perfection and plagued with comparison, it's easy to lose sight of the unique beauty and purpose that God has woven into your very being. We are constantly bombarded with messages that tell us we're not enough—that we need to look a certain way, achieve specific goals, or acquire particular possessions to be valued. Amidst this noise, we often forget a fundamental truth: We are already complete and precious in God's eyes.

For each of us, there is likely some part of God's creation that we are naturally drawn to. For me, it has always been the sky. It's not uncommon for me to drive around to find a better view and to overload the storage on my phone full of sunrise and sunset photos. I sit in awe of God's creation and in awe of His choice to light up the sky in that way. I am profoundly grateful that He does it simply for our delight. I pay close attention to how the colors melt into one another, majestically and almost magically. Then suddenly, the clouds move, or the colors change, and it's majestic again in a whole new way. I remember a moment when I was thanking God for the gift of this world's beauty, and I felt Him remind me that the way I look at the sunrise is the way He looks at me. Why couldn't I accept that I had even more beauty than the things I spent my days admiring? And why was it so hard to believe He feels that way about me? Unfortunately, we live in a world that tempts us to compromise our identity and compare ourselves with everyone else. As we move throughout our day, we often make ourselves smaller than we truly are. Sometimes, we don't even realize it's happening–it's the enemy's favorite trap. Our lives seem to fall apart when we forget who we are and *whose* we are. Maybe not in the moment, but after a pattern of letting the world chip away at our true passions, beliefs, interests, and joy, it becomes harder to recognize ourselves. Compromising our identity may offer momentary satisfaction, but it robs us of joy and purpose long-term. True joy comes from living out our identity in Jesus and fulfilling His purpose for us, which starts with being who we were created to be.

I wish I could say I am immune to this trap, but I'm not. I have to choose to re-embrace my identity intentionally, over and over again. Reclaiming my true self isn't easy, but it is necessary. I have to ask myself hard questions and hear my answers without judgment. I ask myself what I like about who I am and what I like about how I look. I ask myself to consider the moments I'm most joyful and to reflect on what I'm doing and who I'm with in those moments. It results in me choosing to have kitchen dance parties, investing in friendships in new ways, driving with music loud and windows down in the summertime, trying new things and going new places, and even putting myself out there again in the dating realm after years of being single, finally believing I was worth loving. Each small decision brings me back to my authentic, uninhibited, joyful self, and with each step forward, I fall more in love with who God created me to be. It sometimes feels against the grain, but I feel powerful and brave when I choose to take off the lens of the world- the lens of judgment, and instead embrace this idea of being God's masterpiece. I can see now that even the things I didn't love about myself were there for a purpose and could be used for good. I didn't have to earn my spot as God's kid. He created me and chose me before I could even choose Him back. And the same goes for you!

Knowing who we are in Him is crucial to recognize when we compromise ourselves. We can't keep allowing that to happen. It may seem like sticking to our identity is costing us certain friendships, opportunities, etc. Honestly, it will. But the opportunities and relationships God places on our path while we follow Him authentically are way better than the momentary satisfaction and instant gratification from the fleeting things this world tempts our hearts to chase.

What would it take for you to believe that you are God's masterpiece, too?

QUESTIONS TO CONSIDER:

1. What do you love about yourself?

   - Are there things you loved about younger versions of you that somehow were left behind?

2. What things, people, and experiences bring you joy in your life right now? What matters to you? What makes you sad? What prompts you to action?

3. What are you passionate about? How has that passion fueled some of your beliefs, jobs, experiences, leisure, etc?

4. What are some barriers to you being able to embrace yourself fully? The things you like, the things you don't? The things about you that maybe differ from those around you? A lie that is hard to overcome?

5. Reflect on any moments in your life where you realized that the things you previously found your identity in weren't capable of holding you up anymore. Did that prompt you to start looking to Him to define you?

ACTIVITY:

WRITE YOURSELF A LETTER

Write your younger self a letter. Talk about who you are now and what you've overcome. Talk about what you've learned about God and yourself. Reflect on what you want your younger self to continue embodying as she/he ages. Outline the lies that have been easy to believe and give the combatting truth. Then, list a few things you'd like to do to reclaim your identity, re-embrace joy, and become, even more deeply, the you God created.

CHAPTER 15

The Gift of Humility

> *"I am humbled and quieted in your presence. Like a contented child who rests on its mother's lap. I'm your resting child and my soul is content in you."*
> *- Psalm 131:2 (TPT)*

Humility is a very misunderstood concept. Humility is often misunderstood as having a low opinion of oneself, which was my perspective for a long time. I watched as that misunderstood view of humility impacted my self-esteem and confidence. Over time, I have learned that humility is actually having a right view of yourself in relation to God and others. So when I view myself as a child of God, other people as children of God, and God as the loving, infinitely creative, holy, powerful, and compassionately pursuing Father He is, I can rest in that, and both insecurity and pride naturally dissipate. We can be quieted as a result of that humility because when we know who God is and how He views us, we will no longer feel the need to prove that we are worthy and will no longer shrink back in fear of not being enough. Instead, we will be eager to rest with Him and listen.

I love that we are compared to contented children in Psalm 131:2 and reminded that God is a Father. As our Father, He has those same paternal instincts of wanting to calm, protect, and comfort that we often associate with earthly fathers, but to a greater extent.

I have a lot of friends with kids, and I have started being more perceptive about what calms them. As anyone with kids in their lives will know, each child is calmed differently. Some love to be swayed to sleep, some love to be held, some prefer to be wrapped in a blanket, and others like their head stroked. As we spend more time with babies, we learn what comforts them and begin to offer it to them as their source of comfort. God does the same thing with us. He knows us so intimately that He understands exactly what will calm us and bring us contentment, and He does it. But he doesn't do it from afar. He comes close.

Babies do a few things that many of us forget to do as we get older. Or maybe it isn't that we've forgotten, but that we feel we should be able to handle it on our own or that these things make us seem weak.

1. Crying is a baby's way of calling out for help, and collectively, we don't ask for or receive help nearly enough. We choose not to ask for comfort or share our feelings, but God loves when we come to Him and ask Him for what we need.

2. Babies know their mom's voice. Babies can distinguish their mother's voice from other voices, which is wild! I've seen

how quickly children can be calmed when they hear their mother's voice. Even when my friend's toddler is across the room playing and distracted, she looks in that direction when her mom starts talking. Our hearts are like that with God. Our hearts are primed to hear the voice of our Father.

Just as children find comfort and security in their mother's voice, we, too, find peace in recognizing and responding to God's voice. Embracing this truth can reshape how we see ourselves and our relationship with Him. God doesn't want us to view ourselves as lowly. He wants us to fully embrace the wholeness of who He created us to be. There is a sweet middle ground between over-inflating ourselves and striving to be enough. And in that middle ground with God, we find wholeness, contentment, and rest.

QUESTIONS TO CONSIDER:

1. What things/activities/people calm you or make you feel at ease?

2. Think of a time when God calmed you. What did that look like? How did He cater that specifically to you?

3. Think about a situation in which you found it difficult to ask for help or share your feelings with God or with others. What made that difficult? How might your approach change if you embraced the idea that it's okay to seek help and comfort from God and trust in His ability to provide what you need, often provided through the people around you?

4. What do you think could change if you embraced the true definition of humility and embodied it?

ACTIVITY:

HUMILITY SCALE

Look at the humility scale below. Write three words to describe yourself when you feel prideful, three words for how you feel when you're feeling humble, and three when you are feeling insecure. Then gauge your current level of humility, marking it in some way on the scale. Reflect on what it could take to move towards the wholeness and contentment true humility offers. Consider how knowing what you're like in different parts of the scale can help you be proactive in noticing when you're moving to a new space on the scale and how to adjust to move in the direction you want.

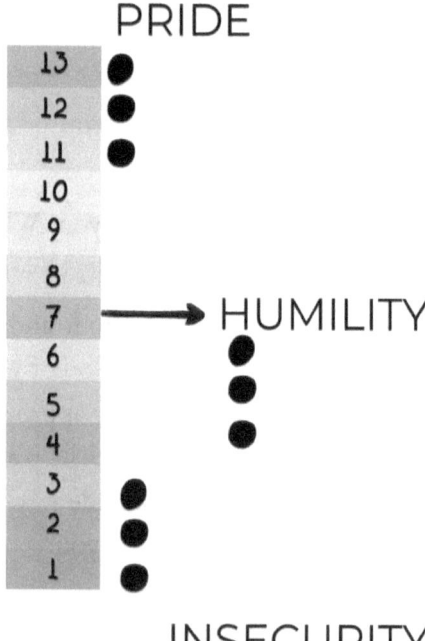

CHAPTER 16

The God of Peace

"You keep him in perfect peace whose mind is stayed on you,
because he trusts in you."
- Isaiah 26:3 (ESV)

I learned recently that young sunflowers turn every day to face the sun. The way these flowers seek the sun contributes to their growth. In maturity, these flowers fix themselves in one stable position.

Like these sunflowers, what we look at matters and contributes to our growth or lack thereof. Looking around this world, it doesn't seem like there is true peace anywhere. We can be easily swept away into the workplace grind, the after-work hustle, the news, or the neighborhood gossip. There is heaviness and unsettledness everywhere. Where is the peace?

When I consider the above words from Isaiah, I immediately notice that peace comes to those whose minds are stayed on the Lord. "Stayed," in this case, literally means for your thoughts to stay or remain in the same place. When we look to God with our minds, eyes, and hearts and stay there, we experience His perfect peace. We only have one mind, so we can't truly fix our minds on the Lord and look all around us simultaneously. Research has proven that multitasking is ineffective and even detrimental because we can't give full attention to either topic. We are presented with the choice to focus wholly on the Lord and see the world through His lens, or focus on the world and miss out on His peace.

When we focus on the world, we see God through the world's lens. That way of living fuels questions and doubts. Where is God? What is He doing? Is He who He says He is? Can He really heal this? Or restore that? Are all things really possible with Him? Can He handle this? Fix that? Is He really working? What's taking so long?- Focusing on God first allows us to see the world through His lens. When we do that, we see everything from a higher perspective. We can remember that He is in control, we can be confident that there is more going on in every scenario than we can see with our eyes, and we can trust the One who is working all things for good.

The choice to trust God enough to look to Him first and stay there might be a massive step for you, and you might not get it right all the time, and that's okay. I surely don't get it right all the time, and frankly, I don't believe there is a "right way"! I feel like I fall short a lot, so if you relate, I want you to know that He delights in our attempts, and the more we choose Him first, the more we'll build the trust it takes to keep staying there and not let the world pull our attention or steal our peace.

My prayer is that we become like sunflowers: reaching tall towards heaven, seeking the light, turning to face the sun, and in our maturity, fixing our eyes there for good.

QUESTIONS TO CONSIDER:

1. What are some things in life that are stealing your peace right now? What are some things that are giving you peace right now?

2. Do you have a rhythm (like the sunflowers) of choosing to turn towards the Son daily?

   • If not, what would it look like to develop that? Can you think of something that would help connect you to Him once (or more) a day?

3. How easy/difficult is it for you to believe that the peace of God is possible to experience in your life? In good times? In struggles?

4. Reflect on a time when you experienced the peace of Christ when it made no worldly sense to feel peace.

ACTIVITY:

FIVE SENSES REFLECTION:

In each column on the first chart, jot down factors that attempt to steal your perfect peace. In the second chart, write about how perfect peace might be experienced through sight, sound, touch, taste, and smell. For me, when I think about feeling at peace, it often looks like dim lighting, early mornings, cozy blankets, a scented candle, and a hot coffee.

Factors That Steal my Peace				
Things I hear	Things I see	Things I taste	Things I smell	Things I touch

Factors That Contribute to my Peace				
Things I hear	Things I see	Things I taste	Things I smell	Things I touch

CHAPTER 17

Embracing God's Promises

> *"For no matter how many promises God has made, they are
> "Yes" in Christ. And so through him the 'Amen' is spoken by us to
> the glory of God."*
> *- 2 Corinthians 1:20 (NIV)*

God is not only a promise maker but a promise keeper. Throughout the Bible, God gives countless promises that we can hold onto because He is faithful to fulfill them. We must spend consistent time in the Word to realize all the promises He has already made to us and learn the character of the One who promised them.

Some of the promises I've been holding onto most recently include:

God will be with me wherever I go (Joshua 1:9).

God will meet all of my needs (Philippians 4:19).

God sustains me (Psalm 55:22).

God has good plans for me (Jeremiah 29:11).

God leads me, protects me, comforts me, and gives me rest (Psalm 23).

God carries my burdens and gives me rest (Matthew 11:28-30).

God is working all things for my good (Romans 8:28).

God's grace is sufficient for me (2 Corinthians 12:9).

God's Word is filled with thousands of promises. But if I'm honest, there have been many times in my life when my reality didn't seem to reflect those promises. I knew His promises were available to me, but I couldn't see them. I couldn't feel them, touch them, or figure out how to embrace them. During those seasons, I realized that I needed to believe before I could see. This isn't just a cliché—until I truly believed that God's promises were for me, I wasn't genuinely looking for them.

To truly seek out a promise, we first need to know what promises God has made and understand what a promise actually is. According to the Collins Dictionary, a promise is "an expressed assurance on which expectation is to be based."[2] This definition highlights the importance of expectation, which is something I feel when I'm certain something is coming.

Many of us experience this feeling of expectation when we know a package we ordered is on its way. There's anticipation as I wait and watch for the truck to pull up. I check multiple times, looking out the window or checking my porch. I have full confidence

---

2 "Promise," *Collins English Dictionary*, HarperCollins, accessed January 31, 2024, www.collinsdictionary.com/dictionary/english/promise.

that the package is arriving, so I'm primed to look for it. Similarly, if I don't believe God's promises are in the process of being fulfilled, I won't be expectantly waiting for them. I won't be prepared to see them, and like a package I didn't know was arriving, it might sit on my porch for days before I recognize it. I might miss it entirely.

Belief prompts us to look for fulfillment. This shift in perspective helps us align our expectations with God's assurances. In doing so, we become more attuned to the ways He is working in our lives, allowing us to fully embrace and recognize His promises when they arrive, because they are everywhere!

If I listed out all the promises God has made to us, I'd be writing for a *long* time. What a gift that is! And because we know that our God is faithful, we can be filled with great expectation. We can choose to live and pray as if all His promises are finding their fulfillment because they are! These are promises we can stand on.

Maybe you're in a place of contentment, adding each promise to your heart like another brick in your foundation of faith. Maybe you're in a place of desperation, needing to grip these promises so tightly and hold onto Him and His Word with all the energy you have left. Wherever you're at, whatever you've done or not done, you are a child of God, and these promises are for you!

QUESTIONS TO CONSIDER:

1. Take some time to explore the promises God has made to you in His Word. Which ones are capturing your attention most today? Why do you think that is?

2. What does it look like practically to intertwine Jesus' "yes" and our "amen"?

3. What are some of the promises God has made to you within your own life?

   - Which of those promises has He fulfilled?

   - Which promises are you still waiting to be fulfilled?

4. What does it look/feel like to let His promises fuel your expectations?

ACTIVITY:

Choose two promises that your heart needs to be reminded of today. If you need help finding them, check the back of your Bible for a glossary. You can look for variations of the word "promise" or even look up specific topics you are struggling with and see what the Bible has to say. The Bible is the best place to start! Write them down and display that paper where you will see it every day this week. When you see it, read it aloud and thank Him for it. The more we internalize the promises of God, the more we will overflow with hope and expectation. We'll begin to live in a way that shows that we are deeply loved by the God who keeps His promises.

CHAPTER 18

Beholding

"And we all, with unveiled face, beholding the glory of the Lord,
are being transformed into the same image from one degree of
glory to another. For this comes from the Lord who is the Spirit."
- 2 Corinthians 3:18 (ESV)

Have you ever seen videos of an artist painting an image? You have no idea what it is or what it will become, but you watch intently, trying to make sense of the colors, brush strokes, patterns, and textures. Then, at the end of the video, the artist flips the painting over, right side up, and you see it immediately. It is a beautiful image, clear as day, making perfect sense. Often, that's what my life feels like. In the process, it makes zero sense. I'm trying to piece everything together, but I can't. I falsely wonder if God is making mistakes, or maybe it's me who just isn't listening enough, following closely enough, or discerning well enough. But then, in God's perfect timing, He flips the whole thing over, and immediately I see it. I see that everything He was doing and allowing was intentional. Every seemingly random brushstroke on the canvas of my life was calculated and made with purpose and intention, with the final product in mind. Just because things don't make sense to us doesn't mean they don't have an essential part in our story, and it surely doesn't mean God made a mistake. There are no accidents in His plan. You are not an accident, and neither is the course your story takes. Biblically, the word "behold" means to fix the eyes upon and observe with care. Most of the time when the word "behold" is used in Scripture, it's to signify that there is more going on than we can see and that what is coming next is vital. That's why we need to observe what God is doing, and how He is moving, with care. I've clung to this word, especially in situations I don't understand. God is always working! In beholding His glory, we are transformed in mind and spirit to be more like Jesus. We may not always see it while we are in the process, but when He finally reveals it to us, it's wild to think we ever could have missed it! It's precisely like these paintings. I can sit in awe of God waiting, beholding Him in the process, knowing that more is going on than I can presently see.

Because God's thoughts are higher than ours and His ways are higher than our ways (Isaiah 55:8-9, NIV), we are often out of the loop on what's really going on in any given situation. What we can do, though, even when we don't understand, is to behold. Some of the ways beholding has looked for me have included:

- Praying for Him to open my eyes to see what He is doing (Ephesians 1:18)

- Journaling a list of 5 things I'm grateful for each day (James 1:17)

- Reading His Word (Psalm 119:130)
- Listening to and singing worship music (Psalms 57:7)

We won't understand what God is doing all the time. As I say that, I'm sure there are plenty of moments coming to mind from your own life that haven't made sense. If, in those moments, we can choose to fix our eyes on the Artist, the Author, and the Father who loves us, then we will find steadiness and peace. If we spend our time getting to know Him and building trust and familiarity with His character, we will gain confidence in knowing that even though we don't understand what He is doing, He will never act outside of His character.

Beholding is to be in awe and to trust the One who always has more going on for our good than we will likely ever know. When we come to the other side and see the picture fully, what a sight that will be to see!

QUESTIONS TO CONSIDER:

1. How can the concept of beholding God's glory and trusting His intentional work apply to your daily life and challenges?

2. Think of a time when you didn't understand what God was doing. How did that feel? Did it ever make you second guess His goodness?

3. As you think about the final reveal of the completed painting in your life, what emotions or thoughts arise, and how does it shape your outlook on the future?

4. How can you cultivate a mindset of awe and trust even when you don't fully understand what God is doing?

ACTIVITY:

ARTISTIC EXPRESSION

Choose a favorite Bible verse related to beholding and create an artistic representation of it. Use calligraphy, doodles, and illustrations to bring the words to life on paper.

CHAPTER 19

Steadiness

"He lifted me out of the pit of despair,
out of the mud and the mire.
He set my feet on solid ground
and steadied me as I walked along."
- Psalm 40:2 (NLT)

I love watching kids learn new things. A few years ago, I distinctly remember my friend's sweet nine-month-old who had just learned to walk. She would run around as far as her little feet would allow, laughing hysterically and having so much fun. She would fall constantly, and almost always, it ended with hitting her head or face off some piece of furniture. I would watch her over and over as this same cycle played out: Run —> Fall—> Cry—> Receive Comfort —> Repeat. Each time after falling, one of us would scoop her up for a few seconds, and then she would be right back to running and laughing again.

Weirdly, I admired her. I admired how she didn't let the hurt, pain, or discouragement of continuing to fall stop her from experiencing the joy of running. She didn't even let those bonks to the head make her fearful and thank God for that because, while she would have avoided countless falls, she would have missed out on all the joy, too. Experiencing joy was worth the risk for her. It's worth it for us, too.

This example was a tangible reminder of how poorly I dealt with the disappointments and pain I experienced in that season. I wasn't always willing to openly express my feelings or let myself receive comfort the way she did. I didn't bounce back the same way she could. I didn't have the determination to keep trying. In some ways, I let it crush me. But I continue to go back to this example because it is also an undeniable representation of how God meets us right in the middle of our disappointments and pain. It is so much easier to let our experiences change how we respond. Whether in the level of risk we are comfortable taking, how big walls become, or how far we allow ourselves to be distanced from hope. But she didn't do that, and in that moment, I felt God wanted that experience for me, too. As the hurt and disappointments come, He comes, too. Scooping us up, holding us, steadying us on our feet, and then it's our turn to decide to take a step and try again. He'll stand right there, arms wide open, calling us to Him, cheering us on, and ready to comfort us when we fall.

As the hurt and disappointments come, He comes, too. Scooping us up, holding us, and steadying us on our feet. Then it's our turn to decide to take a step and try again. He'll stand right there, arms wide open, calling us to Him, cheering us on, and ready to comfort us when we fall

In 2023, one of the words God gave me for the year was "steady." I hoped He meant that my year would have steadiness, ease, and an unshakability, maybe even a clear path forward. That wasn't the case, and as I prayed about it, I realized that the kind of steadiness He wanted to give me came out of the mud and mire. That He could be my steadiness amid shaky circumstances around me. He would be the one I lean on for stability and security in times of uncertainty. That year, my uncertainty looked like dealing with relationships ending, unexpected injuries resulting in canceled plans, and disappointment with job opportunities not panning out. It felt like the big areas of my life were all up in the air. What I learned is that He wasn't promising me that my life circumstances would offer me steadiness. Instead, He was promising me that He would steady me in the midst of my life's circumstances. It's the kind of steadiness my friends offered their sweet girl as she shakily wandered around the room.

As I sought the steadiness He offered, I realized that you don't need to be steadied if you're standing still. When you move, you face obstacles or become off balance and need His steady hand. It takes some action on our part. We must allow ourselves to put down our barriers, step out in faith, take a risk, and then watch Him work.

QUESTIONS TO CONSIDER:

1. Is there an area of your life where the joy and possibility don't seem worth the risk?

2. How does it change your perspective to envision God as a loving Father, arms wide open, cheering you on as you take steps towards where He is calling you, ready at any moment to scoop you up if you fall?

3. Reflect on times in your life when God has steadied you amid shaky circumstances or emotions. What changed in those moments because of Him?

4. What would help you fully trust God's steadiness, and how can you actively cultivate a deeper reliance on His unchanging nature?

ACTIVITY:

EMOTIONAL BAROMETER

Using the image below, indicate how you're feeling right now in mind, body, and spirit. Note how your emotions fluctuate when you feel steadied by God and during times of shakiness. How does that impact your inner state of peace and outward ways of operating in your relationships and the world?

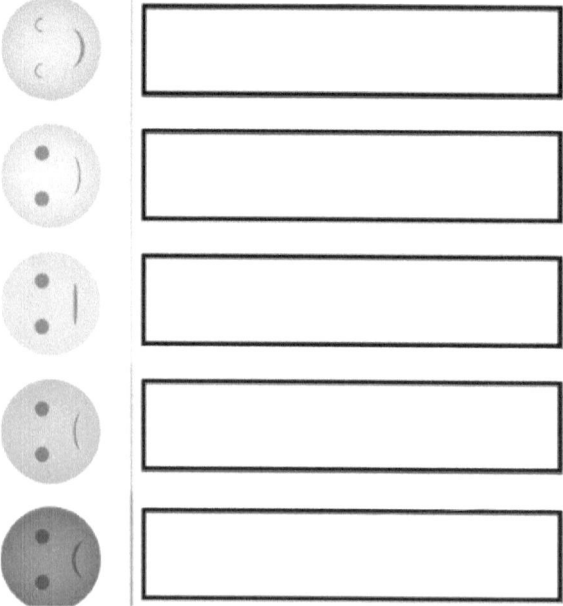

SECTION 2

Unleash

This section of the book focuses on knowing more intimately who God is and how He interacts with and empowers us. Topics in this section will also focus on discernment and knowing/discerning what God is calling us to pursue.

CHAPTER 20

Unleash

In our journey of faith, there comes a moment when God calls us to move beyond merely being released from what holds us back and to step boldly into the expansive freedom He offers. This is the essence of being unleashed. It's not just about shaking off the chains of past limitations, but about embracing the boundless possibilities that lie ahead. When God gives us a word like "unleash," He's inviting us to pursue our divine purpose and to run with passion into the abundance of His plans, just as Paul described in Philippians 3:12.

There are a few different ways the word unleash is typically used or defined in Scripture:

1. To set loose to pursue

2. To free from restraint

3. To allow to move

4. To allow or cause something very powerful to happen

Unleash is a word that has a special place in my heart. Every year I've asked God for a word that would encompass the year to come. Through listening to His Word, and paying attention to themes occurring in my life and in prayer, God gave me the word "unleash" as my word of the year for 2021. It took me a while to determine the significance of this word and how it differed from my word for 2020, which was "release." At face value, they seem interchangeable. I quickly found out they were not. While they are similar in that they both involve letting go, the release has a little more emphasis on being let go *from* something, while the unleashing has a little more emphasis on being let go *into* something. It's simply a change of focus. First, we focused on the things holding us back, and now we focus more specifically on what we are free to run towards.

I have a lot of friends with dogs, and I've seen many of those dogs off-leash. Some are great and stay with their owners, carefully listening to their owner's voice and commands, staying by their side, walking next to them, and when playing fetch, predictably running after the ball and bringing it back. Other friends' dogs (who shall not be named) run away the second their leash is off. They don't listen to commands to stay or to come back. I once had to run for blocks to catch a friend's dog who escaped. Here's the thing about being unleashed: it allows the dogs to pursue what they want. The difference is that the dogs who are good listeners have learned to want what their owner wants. They have learned they are safe, protected, and provided for within their owner's commands. Absolute freedom is found within the bounds their owners have set. The dogs who run away have their own agenda. They are so intrigued by the squirrels and determined to catch them that they don't see the impending danger of the cars. They might be too distracted to realize how far they have veered from home.

God consistently releases us, each time at a new level or in a different way. He spends time teaching me, planting dreams in my heart, and helping me hone my gifts. He speaks to me and calls me to spend more time familiarizing myself with His voice and His ways, so that when He is ready to set me loose into something new, I'm ready. I want to remember those same basic principles when God unleashes me to pursue something. His way is better than mine, and there is protection, safety, and guidance within the boundaries of His commands. I also want to be the one who stays close to Him, listens for His voice, and confidently knows that nothing worth pursuing is worth anything unless He is leading me there.

I felt this way when God planted this dream of writing on my heart. He first led me to discover my own love of reading. Then, He opened doors for me to learn about writing and gave me constant opportunities to practice. He drew me closer to Himself so that I would have meaningful experiences to share, and when I was ready, He set me loose and began running with me on this writing journey. It was freeing to be set on a journey that I hadn't known to plan for. It was all new territory that I didn't know to expect. So everything was new, and there was a delight in the discovery and safety of being a beginner.

Just as freedom allows exploration, may we find our delight in aligning our pursuits with God's purpose. There is so much to explore in these areas that arise as we get older that we likely haven't spent our childhoods dreaming about. Let us choose to navigate the unexpected terrain of life with God as our trustworthy and faithful guide. As we run towards the calling set before us, we can remember that true freedom lies within the parameters of His loving guidance. In every pursuit, may we stay close, listen intently, and find fulfillment in the assurance that the path He leads us on is the path worth pursuing. Let God unleash the fullness of His purpose in your life, and may you run with the passion that only comes from walking hand in hand with Him.

QUESTIONS TO CONSIDER:

1. What does the concept of "unleash" mean to you personally, and how does it resonate with your current life journey?

2. In what ways have you felt restrained or held back in the past, and how does the idea of being unleashed into something resonate with those experiences?

3. Reflect on the idea of experiencing protection and guidance within the boundaries of God's commands. How can you embrace these boundaries to find true freedom in pursuing purpose?

4. Imagine yourself being fully unleashed to pursue your passions. What kind of impact do you envision this having on your life and the lives of those around you?

Activity:

RUNNING MY RACE

Write what you feel God is unleashing you to pursue near the mountains. On the path, write the steps to get there. Write anything you think may distract you from that end goal along the sides where the rocks and bushes are. On the fence, write about the ways God's guidance and boundaries help keep you on track. Reflect on what it would look like to walk this path with God, starting today ... Because you already are!

CHAPTER 21

Connection

"I am the true vine, and my Father is the gardener. He cuts off
every branch in me that bears no fruit, while every branch that
does bear fruit he prunes so that it will be even more fruitful.
You are already clean because of the word I have spoken to you.
Remain in me, as I also remain in you. No branch can bear
fruit by itself; it must remain in the vine. Neither can you bear
fruit unless you remain in me."
- John 15:1-4 (NIV)

P runing is not the first thing that comes to mind when I
think about connection. In fact, it often seems counterintuitive, especially when God prunes the people around us.
I've unfortunately experienced this friendship pruning a handful
of times. Whether by graduating college, moving out of state, or
changing jobs, the people that used to be there for me weren't anymore. Friendships that I thought were for a lifetime were only for

a season. There is pain in that realization, but on the other side of that pain came a level of availability that allowed me to invest my time and energy into the people that were still around. I'd rather have a few deep friendships than a hundred shallow ones. So much more can bloom when we spend our time intentionally nurturing in a few places instead of stretching ourselves to care for too many. This is true of people, but also true of anything that takes our time, attention, and energy.

God created us to be in a relationship with Him and each other. Through those connections, we experience everything God has for us, and we become vessels to give the people around us the things He has for them, too. These connections fuel, nurture, fulfill, and guide us. What we are connected to matters, and God, out of His goodness, promises to cut off connections to things that aren't bearing fruit and prunes other connections so we can be more fruitful. When He does it, though, it doesn't always feel like His goodness. He wants us close to Himself, and when we are close to His heart, we can reflect His heart to others. But we can't reach that level of intimacy with the Lord without some pruning.

I think Jesus used a plant reference in John 15:1-4 for a reason, and when I started searching for information on pruning, I found four primary purposes for pruning, which can give us good insight into reasons God may prune us too:

1. Maintain health by removing the dead or dying parts of the plant.

2. Maintain safety by removing parts that may pose a safety hazard, or that may attach to structures around it that it shouldn't.

3. Growth in a particular direction–gardeners can guide plants to grow to a specific height, width, shape, and fullness.

4. Improve quality. The plant must use its energy to maintain each part of itself: the stem, the buds, the flowers, the fruit, and when a gardener cuts off parts of the plant that are unrelated to its purpose (for example, cutting off the buds of plants that are only used for its leaves), the plant can direct more of its energy to the purpose it is used for.

In the same way gardeners prune certain parts of a plant so the rest can flourish, God prunes pieces of our lives so we can flourish, too. He helps maintain our health by cutting things out of our lives that aren't good for us. He maintains our safety (often without us even realizing it) by directing us away from hazards we don't even see coming and away from relationships or idols He knows we may accidentally attach ourselves to. He trains us in His way and His work, and encourages our growth in a specific direction, running toward His purpose for us. He prunes the things pulling our energy in the wrong direction so we can focus on what He calls us to do.

I can think of instances in my life where God pruned things that weren't inherently bad: small groups, a job, friendships, and opportunities. I had a hard time reconciling how these things that were gifts in one season were no longer good for me. Developing a comfort with letting go enables me to have empty hands, ready to receive whatever God has in store. The difficulty lies in holding onto life loosely so that when God calls for surrender, my hands are unburdened and prepared. I am aware, however, that by anchoring myself solely to Him, my hands will always remain open to His gifts, guidance, and timing, whether in giving or taking away.

What finally shifted my perspective to this looser-grip-on-life type living was repeated pruning in the same places, a constant refining. Through that repeated pruning, I began to see the patterns of fruit: the results of God's constant guidance in the same direction. This pruning looked like adding boundaries around social media and even taking down some of the boundaries around my heart so the people I love can experience the true, vulnerable, messy me. Those weren't all or nothing, immediate decisions. It was a gentle, gradual pruning. It started with taking Sundays off social media, then adding an 8pm cut off time, and has led to phases of entire months off. My vulnerability has also changed. With a few trusted friends, my answer to "How are you?" changed from a constant " I'm good!" to " I'm okay" when that answer felt more true, and now I can often say things like "Today has been pretty good so far. I'm feeling a little anxious today, but I'm looking forward to a bike ride later." It's one gradual level at a time, and the results look like deeper connection, more availability, more intention in fewer places, and more attention on Him and where He wants me.

Pruning can feel scary and confusing, especially when the things He prunes have been a part of our lives for a long time. Sometimes, it feels easier to choose familiarity than to step out into the unknown with Him. Whether it's a job, a lie we've believed, a long-time friend, or a weekly rhythm that God is leading us away from, we can trust that our Gardener knows what He is doing. As He leads you away from certain things and towards new things, we can be sure that these new things are drenched in His love, drawing us nearer to His heart. Through our connection with the Lord, we can be confident that God is good, and His promise to deepen our connection with Him and prune us in that process is a good one, even though it doesn't always feel good. The more we abide in Jesus, the more we will continue to grow in His direction. What a good, good Father we have!

QUESTIONS TO CONSIDER:

1. What does it mean to you to "abide" or "remain" in Him?
   - What are you currently doing to nurture your relationship with the Lord?

2. List your worldly connections (people, opportunities, work, things, etc.)
   - Which of these connections is God continuing to fuel?

3. Can you think of anything recently that God has been pruning?
   - Could that pruning be related to one of those four reasons above? Or something else?

4. Think of an example of a time when God pruned something that you didn't want to be pruned.
   - How did it feel at the moment?
   - Looking back on that moment, what insight can you gain, and where has God led you since?

ACTIVITY:

DRAW A PLANT

Take a moment to engage yourself with God on this topic creatively. Be as creative as you'd like! Get colored pencils, crayons, paint (if you're feeling adventurous), or just your favorite pen. It doesn't have to look good to anyone else's standard. Just enjoy creating a visual representation of what God is showing you here. Say a quick prayer that God will reveal something new and meet you in a fresh way and that, above all, you will feel His heart for you. He loves to meet us when we invite Him!

- Using the top half of a blank sheet of paper, begin to draw a plant. Think of the various parts of a plant–roots, buds, flowers, fruit, stem, branches, etc. Include any parts of the plant that you'd like represented. Imagine that this plant represents pieces of your life right now.

- Think about the different parts of a plant and what they do, and begin labeling them however you see fit. For example, you might label roots with ways you are abiding in the Lord or ways He is nurturing you. You may label fruit or flowers with things He is growing in you or ways His work is already visible in your life. You may choose to have leaves on the ground of things He's already pruned. Maybe there's something new budding. Whatever it is, allow it to be true to you and your life experience.

- When you're done, take a minute to look at your drawing. What do you notice?

- Remember, when God sees you, He sees a masterpiece. Stunning. Blooming. Fruitful. How does it make you feel to know that?

- Now take a few minutes to write a prayer over everything you wrote and drew.

CHAPTER 22

Pursuing Community

"And let us consider how we may spur one another on toward love and good deeds, not giving up meeting together, as some are in the habit of doing, but encouraging one another—and all the more as you see the Day approaching."
- Hebrews 10:24-25 (NIV)

C ommunity plays an indispensable role in our faith journey, and Hebrews 10:24-25 is a beautiful reminder of our calling to foster a loving and active Christian community. However, this hasn't always been an easy endeavor for me. There have been seasons of my life where I've had large groups of friends and regularly scheduled small group, game nights, or some other communal activity. Other seasons of my life have been more isolating and lonely, and I've found it much harder to find a community during those times.

In an effort to seek out or create the kind of community I desire, I've looked to people to know more about it than I do. I've listened to podcasts and read books on the subject, and out of the countless books I've bought on finding godly friends or building community, I haven't opened a single one without fear. Why? Because, if I'm honest with you, I'm scared I'll open them to find that I'm more isolated than I thought, or maybe these books will suggest things I've already tried, and I'll leave feeling more defeated than before. This likely isn't true, but to protect my heart, or probably more accurately, avoid discomfort, I keep those books mostly on the shelf.

I'm realizing that before I can read those books with an open heart and an open mind, there are a few things I can do. First, I can reframe my idea of community and belonging. Would I love to have a group of people who share meals around tables every week, read the Bible together, and have a running text thread for prayers and joys that come up throughout the week? Absolutely! Does the community have to look like that? No. Community can look like neighbors who exchange small talk over the fence and get your packages while you're out of town. It can be a coworker who shares a word of encouragement during a tough day or a family member who listens patiently on the phone. These moments, though they may seem small, are the building blocks of community. They are the tender roots that, with nurturing and time, can grow into the deep, interconnected relationships we long for. We must start by valuing these smaller interactions, recognizing them as significant contributions to our community tapestry.

Secondly, it's crucial to remember that building a community is a journey, not a destination. It's easy to become discouraged when our current situation doesn't match our ideal. Yet, each effort we make in connecting with others, whether a smile, a kind word, or an invitation for coffee, is a step towards the community we aspire to create. God uses these little steps to weave the fabric of community around us and work within us, shaping us into more loving, patient, and understanding individuals. This process may be gradual and filled with ups and downs, but through these experiences, our character is refined, and our relationships are deepened.

Finally, it's essential to lean into vulnerability. The fear of rejection or disappointment can hold us back from reaching out or accepting invitations. However, genuine connections are formed in those moments of vulnerability. Sharing our struggles, asking for help, or simply expressing our need for companionship can open doors to genuine relationships. As we open up, we'll likely find that others are seeking the same depth of community and are willing to walk this path with us.

In essence, the pursuit of community is a journey of small steps, gradual growth, and vulnerability. As we take these steps, let's hold onto the truth of Hebrews 10:24-25, encouraging one another in love and good deeds, building the community we desire, one interaction at a time.

QUESTIONS TO CONSIDER:

1. How do you currently define community, and in what ways might this definition be expanded or altered to include various forms of connections and interactions you encounter daily?

2. Reflect on how you have contributed to building community in the past and how people have initiated that with you. What actions or attitudes were most effective, and what might you do differently in the future?

3. How can being part of a community contribute to your personal growth? Are there aspects of yourself that you could better develop through community involvement?

4. What are three specific, actionable steps (big or small) you can take in the near future to strengthen or expand your sense of community? How will these steps move you closer to the communal bonds you desire?

ACTIVITY:

BUILD COMMUNITY

Pick one thing you can do this week to build community. You could extend an invitation, or you could say "yes" to one. Maybe consider showing up to a group at church or signing up to play cornhole or trivia one evening. Perhaps it's a video call one afternoon or a phone call while you drive. Assess your time and capacity and find an activity that feels good for you and includes someone else. Schedule it! When you're done with that, take some time to journal about what it was like to extend that invitation or take that brave step and how it worked out. Invite God into that and listen for His guidance.

CHAPTER 23

Trusting God's Provision

"And God is able to bless you abundantly, so that in all things
at all times, having all that you need, you will abound in every
good work."
- 2 Corinthians 9:8 (NIV)

In elementary school, my family took a trip out west. It was an eleven-day drive from Pennsylvania to Arizona and back. We stopped at least once in every state we passed, seeing all the notable landmarks. We went a different route home so we would get to see other things. It was a great trip! My parents spent months planning every stop, hotel, activity, and sight-seeing adventure. We saw the Grand Canyon, Lookout Mountain in Colorado, and the St. Louis Arch, among many other things. I had never heard of most of those places before. They weren't necessarily places I would have chosen to visit myself. I probably would have chosen things like Disney World or, frankly, anywhere on an airplane since I thought planes were cool, and there were few things I could think of (besides stops at the Cracker Barrel) that would be fun about being shoved in a car for eleven days.

I mostly remember those things through pictures and stories. But I don't need photographs or stories to remind me of the thousands of times I asked "Are we there yet?" or "How long until we get there?" "When are we going to eat?" " Where are we going to eat?" "Are we sleeping in a hotel?" "How far away is it?" "Does the hotel have continental breakfast?" and "Will I have what I need when I get there?" My parents were gracious in answering my questions at first, although, to be honest, "forty-five more minutes" doesn't mean much to a nine-year-old. After a while, the responses changed to "soon." What I do remember (although I'm confident my parents were annoyed with my persistent questions) is that they always answered me.

But as I reflect on my questions, I recognize that they came from a desire for control and security. I needed to know where we were and where we were going, and information about all the food I would get to eat and when. My parents packed everything ahead of time, so I also wanted confirmation that if we were going on a hike, I had the right boots, and if we were going swimming, someone remembered to pack my swimsuit. I wanted to ensure I'd be taken care of and all my needs would be met. I also was trying to figure out when my waiting would end and I would arrive at these places my parents promised us for months we would go.

So often, I find myself treating life this way, as if somehow my life is a map, and I want to know where we are going, how long until we get there, and if/how my needs will be met along the way. Just as with this trip out west, I'm finding that my parents mirrored for me at an early age what God looks like as we journey through life with Him. Here's what I learned:

1. God always provides for my needs.

2. God is WITH me on the journey. He is not the GPS (which actually didn't exist during this particular trip); He is the driver.

3. The road map is God's responsibility to manage, and He is happy to listen to all of my persistent questions about where we are going and if my needs will be met.

4. God doesn't always give me concrete answers. He might say "soon" or give me a nudge to put something on a list of things I'm praying for for the upcoming year. But rarely does he give me a specific time or date. Most of the time, He asks, "Will you trust me?"

5. We always get where we are going (even if we must reroute a bit), and He faithfully fulfills His promises. Anytime He showed me where we were going, He meant it, and eventually, we arrived.

6. Every time we arrive somewhere, I'm always equipped for the task at hand.

2 Corinthians 9:8 provides me with those reminders over and over again! I know that His blessings are abundant. I am confident that we can count on Him to take us exactly where we need to go, with all the necessary stops along the way. He is the driver on the journey of life and He invites me to travel with Him wherever He leads. If I learn to trust the One who planned this journey, I'll never

need to worry about my needs. I can be sure that God is equipping me every step of the way, providing all I need to accomplish the work He's doing in me, through me, and the work He empowers me to carry out for His kingdom.

QUESTIONS TO CONSIDER:

1. What questions are you currently asking God?

2. Reflect on the root of those questions. What are you looking for? Security? Control? Certainty? Something else?

3. How does reflecting on God's previous provision in your life impact your willingness to step out with Him in new ways, letting Him lead you to new places?

4. Which of the above takeaways is the one you most need to be reminded of? Are there certain situations where you feel this need at a greater capacity? Situations where you are more likely to trust, even when answers aren't ever present?

ACTIVITY:

DRAW A MAP

Draw a map reflecting either your past year's adventures or the upcoming adventure you feel God is leading you on. Begin with a brief reflective session, pondering your journey's highs and lows and outlining your questions for God. Craft a visually symbolic map, integrating your questions and perceived answers. Think about how God equips you and has equipped you in the past. Document any significant milestones and noteworthy growth you've made along the way. *Hint: all growth towards God is noteworthy, no matter how "big" or "small" you (or others) perceive it to be.

Feel free to use the illustration below as a guide.

Then, step back from your completed map and reflect on it as a "bigger picture" version of what you are currently living out, recognizing that it is all in His hands.

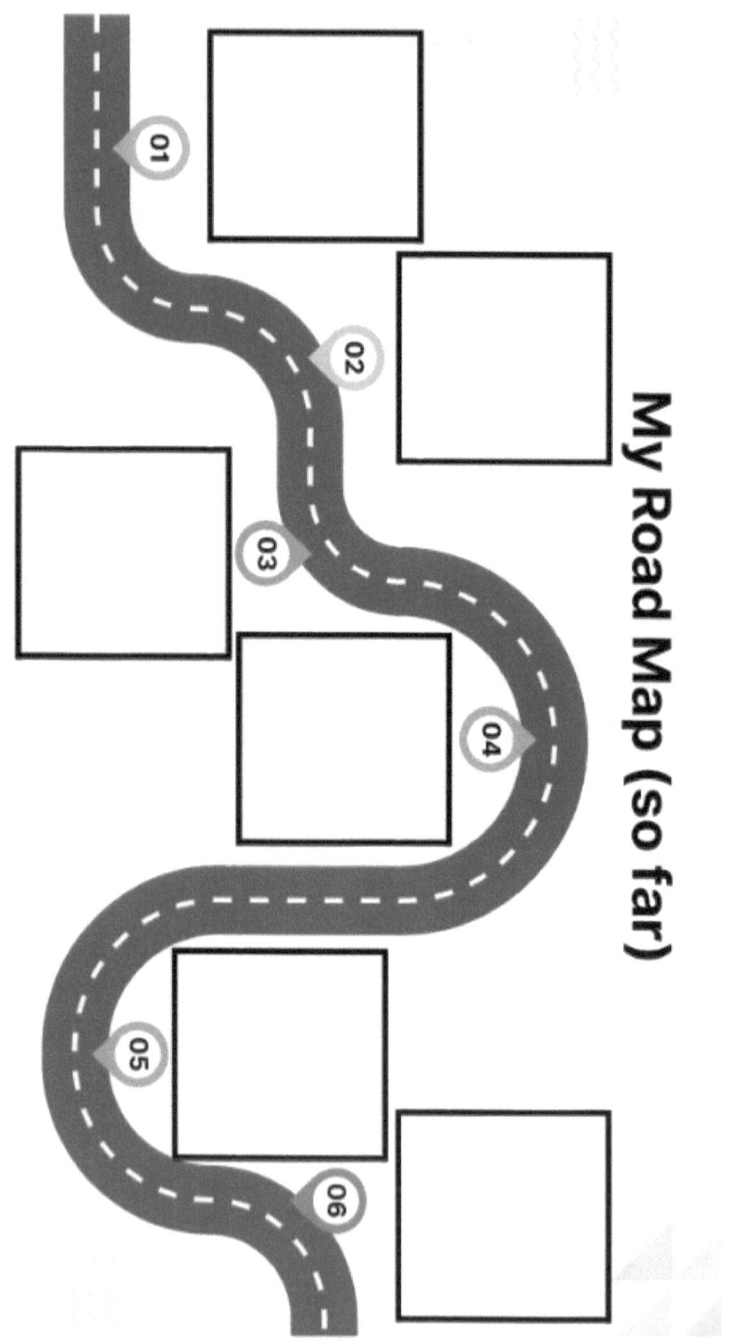

My Road Map (so far)

CHAPTER 24

Seeking God's Wisdom

> *"If you need wisdom, ask our generous God, and he will give it to you. He will not rebuke you for asking."*
> *- James 1:5 (NLT)*

As I sit with a career decision, I fear the future. I fear what it may require me to give up or the people that may fade from my life because of it. I fear the way my life could change. It's messy and complicated. I second guess, overthink, pray, and cry. I wrestle with it all. In that fear, I feel shaky. But that shakiness makes me think that maybe I've been holding on so tightly to something that is no longer worth my grasp. God's call to move on is clear, but everything else is as clear as mud. I'm left with questions and uncertainty about my circumstances. I need wisdom.

So many aspects of my life revolve around my work. My purpose, my inspiration, my friendships, social opportunities, and my finances. Letting go of a job that has so many other aspects intertwined is hard. Honestly, "hard" seems like an understatement, but it's necessary to let go of things in our lives, especially when we feel God is leading us to do so. Sometimes, we need to empty our hands before we are free to receive something new. I want open hands and the freedom that comes along with that.. Yet what I'm already holding feels familiar, predictable, and comfortable. Familiarity can trick us into feeling a sense of security. Having empty hands feels scary and has me asking questions like, "What will God give me to hold next?" "Will it feel like a breath of fresh air? Will it be confusing, or will it be clear?" "How long will my hands be empty and my heart be longing to hold something new?"

We all go through times like this, where things are unclear, and we don't know what to do. In those moments of doubt and questioning, there's one thing I'm certain about: God is infinitely wise! And we have access to that wisdom through Him. He doesn't expect us to have it on our own, but He offers it generously if and when we ask. And I would much rather ask and go where God leads me than anywhere else. So, I'll take that leap of faith with Him because I truly know and love Him. It might feel risky, but making decisions based on His guidance is where my ultimate security is found.

I've come to understand that seeking God's wisdom is not just about receiving answers, although He loves to answer us! It's about developing a deeper relationship with Him. This relationship is built on trust, a trust that He knows what is best for me, even when the path seems daunting. I've realized that surrendering my plans, fears, and desires is not a sign of weakness, but rather, a bold step of faith and an opportunity to invite Him to share His plan with me. In this surrender, I have access to the peace of knowing that God's plans for me are far greater than anything I could imagine for myself. As I stand at this crossroads in my career, I find comfort in the promise that He is with me, guiding each step. Along the way, He provides His wisdom- through Scripture, people, prayer, and life's experiences. Jesus tells us that the Holy Spirit is our "Paraclete," from the Greek word "paraklētos," meaning Helper, Advocate, Encourager, and Friend.[3] We can rely on Him to be all of those things and more.

The more I focus on who He is, the less I fear the path He's leading me on. If we can trust the guide, the path doesn't matter. I no longer have to worry about the terrain I'll encounter or if I have all the right equipment and skills to reach the destination. Instead, I can trust that He knows best and will show me where to go and what I need. Each day is an opportunity to grow in faith and to witness how God can turn my fears and doubts into a story of grace and purpose. In this journey of seeking God's wisdom, I'm not just finding answers; I'm finding myself transformed and renewed in His love.

I learn to lean in and say "yes." I learn to cling to hope and cling to the One in whom my hope is found. When life feels messy, I turn to the One who makes order out of chaos, not as a last resort, but as a first response, because the God who loves me is faithful. He's faithful in my questioning. He's faithful in my doubt. He's faithful every single day, and my hope is found in Him.

---

3 Strong, *Strong's Concordance*, 3875.

QUESTIONS TO CONSIDER:

1. How do you balance the fear of the unknown with the trust in God's wisdom and plan for your life?

2. Can you recall a time when seeking God's wisdom led you to a decision or path you wouldn't have chosen on your own? What was the outcome?

3. How does the concept of the Holy Spirit as a Helper, Advocate, Encourager, and Friend manifest in your life? How can you connect with Him for wisdom in your daily decisions?

4. Is there any particular area of your life where you're struggling to let go of your ways/ ideas/plans to allow God to show you His instead?

ACTIVITY:

PRAY

Pick one area of your life where you need God's wisdom. Pray about that each day and record anything you hear from God or others on that topic in the illustration below. Take note of any specific Scriptures, thoughts, or songs that come to mind while praying, and consider those among the many ways God will try to reach you and respond.

Sunday	Monday	Tuesday	Wednesday	Thursday	Friday	Saturday

CHAPTER 25

Patience and preparation

"My fellow believers, when it seems as though you are facing nothing but difficulties, see it as an invaluable opportunity to experience the greatest joy that you can! For you know that when your faith is tested it stirs up in you the power of endurance. And then as your endurance grows even stronger, it will release perfection into every part of your being until there is nothing missing and nothing lacking."
- James 1:2-4 (TPT)

When I eat pizza rolls fresh out of the oven, I always know I should wait until they cool off, but they are delicious, and I'm usually hungry. So naturally, as many of us do, we risk the burn and take a bite. I remember one particular instance when they burned my mouth so badly I couldn't taste anything for a few days afterward.

As I was thinking about patience one morning, God brought this example back to mind and showed me how it works similarly with Him. God gives us promises and He has our lives marked for specific works. Even though it's part of His plan for us, if we pursue those things prematurely, what was meant to delight us and fulfill us burns us instead. Not only are we prevented from experiencing that thing in its fullness, but we also are prevented from tasting the other good things God has for us. There are ripple effects to our own impatience. But there is a purpose to the wait!

Waiting seasons are a challenging test of our faith. But as the verse above shows, it's precisely that difficulty and testing that allows us to experience joy, to build endurance, and to be perfected. I'm in a waiting season right now. I'm betting that if you aren't in one now, you will be at some point, so I don't want you to miss this. This is important. I spent many years of my life not knowing crucial things about waiting seasons. These days, I'm more of a regular in waiting seasons than I am in my local coffee shop, and I've learned a few things along the way that I want to share with you.Consider your current waiting season or one you've been in recently, and explore the following ideas:

Wait *with* God, not *for* something.

It can be easy to spend waiting seasons focused on the things we're waiting for instead of focusing on the One we're waiting *with*. If we are waiting, we are clearly waiting *for* something, but what if we let our focus shift from the blessing to the blesser?

Waiting isn't wasted.

Waiting can feel like a waste sometimes. If God is going to bless me with a house (for example), does it matter if He does it now or two years from now? In my mind, no. But God is working in our waiting. Maybe He has something for me and you right here in the middle of the wait. Psalm 84:11 says, "No good thing will He withhold from those who walk uprightly." Let that sink in. God isn't withholding from you. There's a reason for this wait, and I believe that whatever the reason, it's for your greatest good and His greatest glory.

QUESTIONS TO CONSIDER:

1. How can God uniquely meet you when you are waiting that maybe He can't in another season?

2. What are you learning about God as you wait?

3. Is there something you need to learn or a characteristic that needs to develop in you that is necessary before reaching the end of your wait?

4. How can you grow closer to God and lean in during this waiting season instead of trying to speed through it?

ACTIVITY:

MIND MAP EXPLORATION:

Using your answers above, create a mind map as a visual reminder of why your waiting matters and what you can do and learn while you wait. Starting with the central theme of "Patience and Preparation," branch out with keywords, thoughts, and reflections connected to this theme.

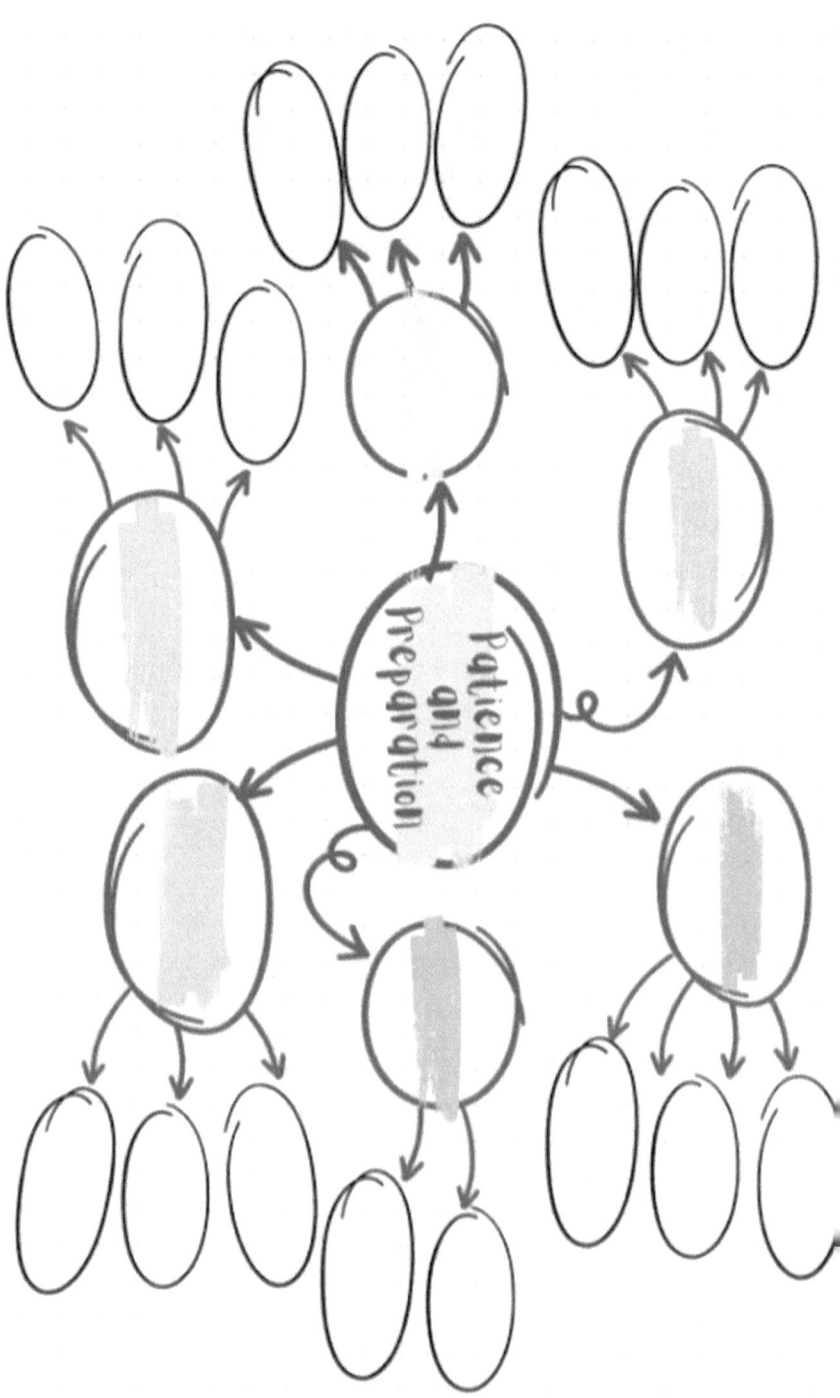

Patience and Preparation

CHAPTER 26

Building a Habit of Creativity

"You are worthy, our Lord and God, to receive glory and honor and power, for you created all things, and by your will they were created and have their being."
- Revelation 4:11 (NIV)

When you meet new people, you often tell them your name and give them a description of who you are. You might say, "Hi, I'm Megan, the author of Clinging to the Vine." Or "I'm ____'s mom," or "I work at _____." We all have some quick way of giving people an idea of who we are. How you introduce yourself often changes based on the setting because you want to highlight a connection point. So, when I look at how God introduces Himself to us, I wonder if He was doing the exact same thing: telling us an aspect of who He is and highlighting a connection point between us.

The first thing we learn about God is that He is a creator. Genesis 1:1 says: "In the beginning, God created..." God is infinitely creative, and His creativity isn't one-dimensional. He created us, His people, with all of the human body's intricacies, and He also created emotions, mountains, and beautiful sunrises. Our lives and our world are full of His creativity, and because we are made in His image, we are creative people, too. Our creativity does not have to be one-dimensional, either. There is no specific mold. Our creativity, in whatever form, takes root in the creative nature He gave us, and in every creative endeavor, we get to emulate Him.

With this in mind, I had to shift my view of creativity to discern what it looks like for me. It turns out "creativity" isn't synonymous with "artistic." Instead, it's more about bringing something into existence. In this way, not only is that a connection point with God, but an opportunity He gives us to offer people visible, tangible, sensory experiences of His creativity overflowing within us. While I create, I pause and invite God to join me there, remembering that creating is Holy work. It's something set apart and connective, and both the process and the product can glorify God.

Whether you're creating a latte or creating a business, writing a book or writing an encouraging text, building a cabinet or building community, painting a mural or painting a kitchen, making music or making dessert, it all matters. What you create and the way you create matters! And the most amazing part is that there will never be a moment when the world doesn't have space for what you have to offer! Read that again. There is space for you and for the things you create!

The truth we must embrace is that our creativity is as unique as our fingerprints—no one can create in the exact way we do, nor can they replicate the singular blend of experiences, emotions, and perspectives we bring to our work. When we compare, we overlook the value of our individuality, the essence that makes our creations special and needed in the world. Instead of looking sideways, let's look within and upwards. Let's draw inspiration from our lives and our Creator, recognizing that each stroke of a brush, each word penned, and each melody composed is a testament to our distinctiveness and an arrow pointing directly to God. By celebrating our unique creative voices and resisting the urge to compare, we honor ourselves and the Divine, who delights in our creativity and fills our world with light and joy as we collectively bring our creative offerings. It is your uniqueness that the world craves, and when we show up and create in whatever way we do, we make this world a brighter and more beautiful place.

Our masterfully creative God places unique gifts and passions inside us and constantly moves our souls to create. We partner with God in sacred work as we lean into those creative gifts. I'm not sure what you're creating or hesitating to let yourself create, but know this: the world needs it! And the more we do it, the more we can access that connection point with God. I encourage you (as I equally encourage myself) to create something. While you do it, pause for a moment to remind yourself that it matters.

QUESTIONS TO CONSIDER:

1. What are ways you enjoy creating or have enjoyed creating in the past?

2. What are ways you feel pulled to create but are hesitating to allow yourself the opportunity? What barriers are you experiencing?

3. When comparison rises within you, how can you compassionately acknowledge it, confront it, submit it to God, and move through it, reminding yourself that no one creates exactly like you?

4. How has creativity been a connection point with God in the past? If you haven't experienced that yet, consider ways to invite Him into future creative processes.

ACTIVITY:

AGENDA

Use the sample agenda below to schedule a time to be creative in whatever form feels authentic for you. Write a prayer to invite God into this time with you. Before you do that creative project, go back to this page and pray the prayer you wrote. Then go emulate Him!

Sunday	Monday	Tuesday	Wednesday	Thursday	Friday	Saturday
Date: Time: Creativity:	Date: Time: Creativity:	Date: Time: Creativity:	Date: Time: Creativity:	Date: Time: Creativity:	Date: Time: Creativity:	Date: Time: Creativity:
Prayer:	Prayer:	Prayer:	Prayer:	Prayer:	Prayer:	Prayer:

CHAPTER 27

Cultivating a Heart of Joy

"Because I set you, YAHWEH, always close to me, my confidence will never be weakened, for I experience your wraparound presence every moment. My heart and soul explode with joy— full of glory! Even my body will rest confident and secure."
- Psalm 16:8-9 (TPT)

The word "explode" immediately captures my attention. It often has a negative connotation. Exploding with anger. Exploding with impatience. Exploding with frustration.

Exploding with joy, though? That isn't my first thought, but that is precisely the picture Psalm 16:8-9 is painting. And that sounds like something I want!

Whatever we let build up inside us explodes when we are put under pressure, and whether we want it to or not, it scatters fragments everywhere. If we are full of joy, peace, and the love and light of Jesus, when we explode, we will scatter that in every interaction, with every person, everywhere we go. If our hearts explode with fear or anger, we can spread fragments of that, too. I've been on the receiving end of both types of explosion, and while neither are inherently bad, I definitely prefer scattering joy.

Picture an explosion of joy like a magnificent fireworks display. Just as a firework bursts forth in a dazzling array of colors, lighting up the night sky, our hearts can also explode with radiant joy. Just as a firework cannot be ignited without a flame, our joy finds its spark in our nearness to the Father. The beauty of this explosion is not merely confined within us; it is designed to be shared. When our hearts are filled with the joy of the Lord, it becomes a captivating spectacle for others to witness and experience, spreading joy like a contagious celebration.

Our starting point: being close to the Lord, confident, unshakable, and surrounded by His presence. The result: our hearts and souls explode with joy, and our body rests confident and secure.

It would be a mistake to end here and not acknowledge the beauty of that statement in Psalm 16:9: "Even my body will rest confident and secure." If you're anything like me, I didn't even consider my body when I read the other parts of that verse. The words "unshakable" and "confident" seem to refer to our minds, and I believe the author anticipated this interpretation. He then specifically mentions our bodies, reminding us that they are included as well. I hadn't realized that joy could be a full-body experience. What a gift that every part of us can wholly and entirely be secure in Jesus because of His presence and the gift of His explosive joy!

QUESTIONS TO CONSIDER:

1. What is joy, and how do you typically experience it?
   - Is it ever an experience including mind, body, and spirit?

2. Take some time to look up the Biblical definition of joy. Does your definition of joy match the Biblical definition? How does it differ?

3. Think of someone in your life that is particularly joyful. Describe this person. Why do you think they are so joyful? How does their joy impact you? (Consider sharing that with them if you feel led to do so.)

4. Why do you think joy results from our intentional choice to be close to God and choose to recognize His nearness?

ACTIVITY:

Engage with the image below in whatever way you choose. Label things, color them, write all over them, or whatever feels creative and tactile. As you do, reflect on some of the things building up inside you, the things or people igniting an explosion, what is exploding, or maybe what you wish was exploding instead, who is witness to the explosion, etc.

CHAPTER 28

Cultivating a Heart of Gratitude

"Do not be anxious about anything, but in every situation, by prayer and petition, with thanksgiving, present your requests to God."

- Philippians 4:6 (NIV)

I created my Hope Shelf during a tumultuous period marked by the global onset of COVID-19. I was searching for a house when the world around me seemed to spiral into chaos, and the housing market became incredibly uncertain. I'd love to say my faith wasn't shaken, but I can't. I found it so difficult to reconcile my anxiety with the fact that I was hearing God tell me to buy a home, be a neighbor, and put down roots. I believed wholeheartedly that God had a home out there for me. I yearned for a tangible symbol to represent this belief because, honestly, the numbers weren't adding up. Experts' opinions on the trend of the housing market didn't align with what I could afford, and without a tangible reminder of what God said to me and what I was praying for, I was afraid I'd give up hope.

That tangible symbol came in the form of a mug I bought that says "New Home, New Adventures." While it may be just a mug to some people, it wasn't just a mug to me; it was a declaration of my faith, a tangible representation of my belief, and a visual symbol of my hope for a home. When I moved into my next apartment, which wasn't my plan at all, I put this mug under my bed, hoping that someday I would get to use it. As I reflected on this with God, I got the idea to buy some other small tangible reminders of the other things I was praying and believing for.

I shared this idea with a friend. Without missing a beat, she said, "If you really believed God would come through, wouldn't you display them on a shelf instead of hiding them under your bed?" Ooof! She was right. I got a shelf and filled it with small representations of the big things I believed God would do. This was my way of presenting my requests to God and thanking Him in advance for all He was doing. And it's not just a shelf for me. There are dreams on that shelf and reminders of ways I'm praying for the people I love–for their God-sized dreams, their hope, and their healing. It's not about the items at all. It's about a little nugget of faith that says, "I will buy this mug because one day, I'll use it in my new home." It's the hope-filled step of purchasing a onesie I believe my child will wear one day. It's a picture of a food my friend will one day enjoy without an allergic reaction. It's my prayers in tangible form. I pray over these things and people daily, but displaying them for all to see is still scary. Yet, that's faith; vulnerable, authentic, and open wide for people to see.

I believe in and deeply love a big God, and all things are possible for Him!

QUESTIONS TO CONSIDER:

1. What ways do you practice gratitude for the things God has already done?

2. How does it feel to thank God for things He has yet to do?

3. Do you have a way of sharing or showing your faith-filled prayers? If not, what would it look like to display your hope in a tangible way?

4. Can you recall a specific instance where expressing gratitude led to a noticeable change in your attitude or situation? If so, how did this experience impact your faith?

ACTIVITY:

HOPE SHELF

If you had a hope shelf, what would be on it? Use the illustration below to reflect on that question.

CHAPTER 29

Embracing God's Grace

"But he answered me, "My grace is always more than enough
for you, and my power finds its full expression through your
weakness" So I will celebrate my weaknesses, for when I'm weak,
I sense more deeply the mighty power of Christ living in me. So
I'm not defeated by my weakness, but delighted! For when I feel
my weakness and endure mistreatment—when I'm surrounded
with troubles on every side and face persecution because of my
love for Christ, I am made yet stronger. For my weakness becomes
a portal to God's power."
- 2 Corinthians 12:9-10 (TPT)

I have spent weeks in 2 Corinthians 12, dissecting it piece by piece. One of my favorite things about God's grace is that it's a free gift. Completely free. It's such a miraculous promise that I can't wrap my head around it. I'm so used to hearing these verses in other versions that I became desensitized to it. Then I landed on this verse from The Passion Translation, which brought new light to familiar words. I then started approaching God with questions. Why is this Your design? What would compel You to do this for us? How does it work? What part do I play?

I wasn't sure what to do with all of these questions, so I took the verse word by word, dissecting it, looking up definitions and cross-references and every ounce of information I could that would help me see a fuller picture of what God is offering us here. I realized that if this was what God had available for me, I wanted to receive it, but I wasn't sure how.

I took my questions to my journal as I peeled the layers of this passage apart, one by one. Exploring verses this way has been hugely helpful in new revelations and discovering God's truth, as it was originally written in Hebrew, Greek, or Aramaic. There are so many tools at our disposal, things like footnotes, different Bible translations, Bible dictionaries and commentaries, that shed new light on familiar verses and unlock understanding that I didn't know was possible. This is the gift of God's Word being the living Word. There will always be more to discover. There were a few things that struck me in this practice. First, the footnotes in The Passion Translation compare God's presence to a tabernacle or shelter, places we go for help, rest, and protection. This is absolutely true of our faith. God is the one who provides help, rest, and protection, not just after our trials, but within them, too. I love that the shelter He provides isn't outside our circumstances because it shows we don't need to earn protection or overcome our situations to deserve rest. We don't have to run from what we are dealing with to find what we need most. We don't need to search for shelter; God brings shelter to us. The part I play is to receive it. I get to trust that before the situation is resolved, I can rest. When I admit my weakness, I can access God's power. The more I try to work things out for myself, the less room I give God to work.

The next thing that struck me was the word "surrounded," which means "to encircle so as to cut off communication from someone/something." In my mind, I envisioned myself standing at the center of an enormous circle, completely encircled by adversaries and overwhelming challenges, feeling cut off and isolated. In hindsight, it's clear that isolation is exactly what the enemy wants for us. The enemy wants to get close to us, whispering lies, distracting us, and attempting to separate us from God. But when God's presence breaks through, coming in to rest on us like a tabernacle, joining us within our troubles, He covers us and surrounds us. In doing that, He becomes the closest thing to us, not our troubles. As He surrounds us, He becomes the barrier between us and the enemy, cutting off the ways he is trying to communicate with us. We no longer hear the ringing of the enemy's lies because God is closer. His voice is louder. Communication with the Lord can never be cut off. God is so powerful and loving and kind that He cuts us off from evil, but no power can ever cut us off from the love and presence of God.

Exploration of these verses led me to a deeper understanding of what God does for us in times of difficulty, and now that I know it, I look for it. As I look for it, I see it. And as I see it, I feel it. I didn't know to look before. These are good promises, ones you can hold onto! Because we will have trouble, but our God has overcome it all.

Here is a little excerpt of what my journal looked like as I dissected this verse and the meaning of the words within it.

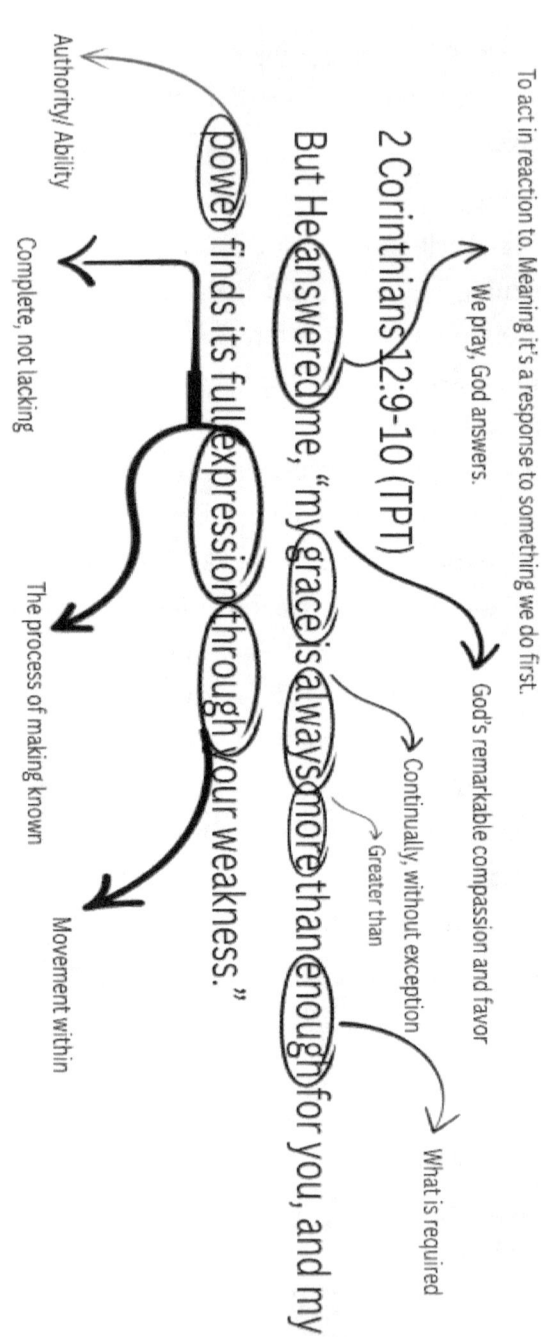

To act in reaction to. Meaning it's a response to something we do first.

We pray, God answers.

God's remarkable compassion and favor

2 Corinthians 12:9-10 (TPT)

But He answered me, "my grace is always more than enough for you, and my power finds its full expression through your weakness."

Continually, without exception

Greater than

What is required

Authority/ Ability

Complete, not lacking

The process of making known

Movement within

1. What are you surrounded by right now?

2. What do you experience when God joins you in the middle as your shelter?

3. How does this change your perspective on times of difficulty and reframe moments of weakness as an opportunity for God's strength to shine?

4. What is something new you discovered as you explored this verse?

   - Take a moment to thank God for His living, breathing Word and for anything He has revealed to you through it.

When I'm surrounded with troubles on every side

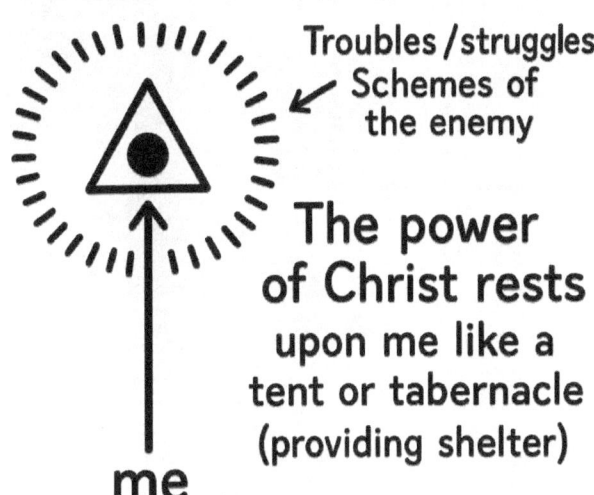

Troubles / struggles
Schemes of
the enemy

The power
of Christ rests
upon me like a
tent or tabernacle
(providing shelter)

me

ACTIVITY:

Label anything that comes to mind. Consider what it looks and feels like to be surrounded. How can this image be a reference point for you in future times of difficulty?

CHAPTER 30

The Lord Refines Me

*"These trials will show that your faith is genuine. It is being
tested as fire tests and purifies gold—though your faith is far
more precious than mere gold. So when your faith remains strong
through many trials, it will bring you much praise and glory
and honor on the day when Jesus Christ is revealed to the whole
world."*
- 1 Peter 1:7 (NLT)

Talking about being refined and purified isn't the most comfortable thing, and I get it. It doesn't often *feel* comfortable, either. We all love the results of testing and refinement, but let's be honest—none of us actually enjoy the process. Here's the thing: God's actions are always for our good. So, maybe it's worth asking the hard questions to figure out why our refining process matters so much.

My understanding of refinement evolves with my life stage, circumstances, and intimacy with God. However, it often returns to a consistent theme: how I utilize my time. It started with setting aside ten minutes each morning to read the Bible and pray. Since then, it has evolved into questions around what shows I watch, whether I read a book or scroll, whether I do housework on Sunday or let myself rest. And a big one: do I spend my time running from my emotions, suppressing them, numbing myself and pretending I'm fine, or do I get the courage to say "I'm not okay" or "I'm lonely" and actually bring my feelings to God and others in an honest, whole-hearted, and vulnerable way? At the end of the day, I can't heal from things I don't admit exist. I can't allow myself to process things and live a fully embodied life if I don't make space for that.

These things, as simple as they may seem at surface level, continue to challenge my faith. Resting when there is work to be done requires me to trust that God will help me get it all done. Choosing to read instead of scroll produces growth in me that getting lost on social media never could. Choosing to tell someone how I really feel opens me up to a level of love that cannot be experienced otherwise, but it also forces me to surrender and trust that I won't be met with rejection, or if I am, that God still has meaningful friendships and deep connections available for me. The more I do these brave things, the easier that bravery becomes.

In 1 Peter 1:7, our faith being tested is compared to how fire purifies gold. That analogy holds some profound truths that we should explore further:

Gold's Indestructibility: Gold cannot be destroyed. It can be melted and formed but does not rust, tarnish, or become discolored. Similarly, when our faith goes through testing, it is not destroyed but is formed. The very essence of our faith remains unbroken and unyielding.

Purging Impurities: Fire pulls out impurities from gold. In the same way, God strengthens and purifies us through testing. Our challenges serve as a refining fire, extracting impurities from our lives and character.

God's Gift of Faith: Gold cannot be created; it is a gift from God. Our faith works similarly. God is the Author and Originator of our faith. It is built, formed, purified, and strengthened, but it cannot be created out of our own strength or ability. It's a divine gift, a reflection of God's grace.

The Reflective Nature of Gold: The goldsmith knows that the gold is purified when he can see his own reflection in it. Likewise, God is continually purifying and perfecting our faith until He looks at us and sees a reflection of Himself. Our journey through testing and refinement is a process that aligns us with the image of God.

Why does this refining process matter so much? Because our faith is precious to God, and in a beautifully backward way, the heat of the fire is the sign of a skilled craftsman who is fully invested in forming our faith. God is nurturing us and shaping us toward perfection, and the result is a reflection of His glory.

When we face trials, it's essential to remember that God's interest in refining us is not to break us down, but to build us up. The discomfort we experience is not meant to harm us, but to mold us into vessels that can carry the weight of His glory. Just as a sculptor chips away at a block of marble to reveal a masterpiece, God, in His infinite wisdom, chips away at our imperfections, revealing the beauty of our true selves.

Each trial and every challenge we encounter contributes to the ongoing process of shaping us into individuals who reflect the character of God. It's a journey marked by resilience, endurance, and an ever-deepening trust.

The next time you find yourself in the refining fire, remember that it's a testament to God's investment in your spiritual formation. Embrace the process, knowing that you are not alone in the fire; the Master Craftsman is with you, carefully sculpting a faith that will endure, shine, and ultimately bring glory to His name. Your faith is not just a commodity; it's a masterpiece in the making, a testament to the enduring love and transformative power of the One who holds you in His hands.

Questions to Consider:

1. Why is your faith so precious to God?

2. What aspect of this gold and fire metaphor speaks to you?

3. Why do you think trials and testing are the avenues for refinement and purification?

4. Do you feel God's nurturing and skillful hand during your trials? If so, how? If not, how can you fix your eyes more fully on Him amidst the fire?

Activity:

FAITH TIMELINE

Sketch a visual representation of your spiritual journey. Draw a timeline with critical milestones, challenges, and moments of growth. Take some time to reflect on what you've drawn.

CHAPTER 31

The Lord Delights in Me

Wﻓhen I dive into so many deep topics in a row, as we have been in this book, I sometimes end up with more "to-do" lists—more steps I need to take or moves I need to make to practically apply what I'm learning. I'm confident God wants us to know Him more. He invites us to learn, grow, and become more accurate reflections of Jesus, but sometimes that growth can feel overwhelming. In those moments, I need to pause and remember the most important thing—the inception and epicenter of my faith: God's love for me.

Yes, He shows us how to live, and He shows us the way we should go. He gives us tools that we get to put into practice to become even more devoted followers. All that is true. But, following Jesus isn't a perpetual cycle of Him weighing us down with rules to follow or burdening us with "shoulds".That's not who He is, and the more we know Him, the more our desire to follow Him is fueled by our love for Him rather than our rule-following tendencies or our fear of consequences.

The more I spend time in His Word, the more I notice Him in my life too. And the more I see His hand in my everyday life, the more I realize I am safe with Him and that the ways He guides me are because they lead to abundance, even if they feel more like a boundary. I don't have to be afraid, because He is with me and He works it all out for my good.

God wants growth for us, but He doesn't love that future, wiser, more evolved version of us any more than He loves us right now. He loves you exactly as you are in every stage of life. More than anything, God wants YOU. Humans were created for a relationship with God. Jesus died on the cross in pursuit of repairing our fractured relationship with Him and closing the distance between us forever. God is always pursuing you because He loves you. He created you on purpose. Your personality, your body, your gifts, the things you like about yourself, and the things you don't. It all makes up who you are, and you are precious to Him. Whatever your life looks or feels like–your highs and lows, smooth sailing, or crumbling mess, He is in it all with you because He loves you. He delights in you! He celebrates with you, comforts you, provides for you, hears you, speaks to you, and rejoices over you. All because of love.

I encourage you to take today to focus on that, too. He doesn't just love you; He likes you. Even more than that, He delights in every detail of your life. He rejoices over you with joyful songs and has countless thoughts about you. Yes, YOU! So today, soak in His goodness and His grace. Let Him pour His love out on you and speak to you about all the ways He delights in you. Because everything else we do gets to flow out of a place of knowing that God deeply loves us.

ACTIVITIES:

HAVE A CONVERSATION.

Make a list of things you love about yourself and that you believe God loves about you. Think about the moments you've felt most loved and delighted in by Him, then engage with God on all those things. Share with Him anything these verses stir up in you... areas where you can feel His delight and where you may struggle to love yourself or receive His love. Write down that conversation. Write your words in one color, and when you feel God responding, write what you hear in another color.

PICK A FRIEND.

Pick someone in your life (or more than one person if you have the time). List out some ways that you recognize them as His masterpiece. Ask God to reveal ways He delights in them and share that with them.

DELIGHT WITH GOD.

Pick one activity you can do with God today that brings you (and Him) delight. Maybe it's a dance party, car karaoke, a walk, cooking, cozying up on the couch with your family, reading a book, or anything that brings you joy. If it brings you true joy, know that

He is in it, and it brings Him joy too. He loves to see you smile and laugh. All good things are from the Lord!

QUESTIONS TO CONSIDER:

1. Was there anything in your conversation with God that surprised you?

2. Was there anything He said that your heart needed to hear?

3. Do you feel unconditionally loved and deeply delighted in by God?

   • If you're not there yet, what would it take to fully believe that God delights in you precisely as you are right now?

4. What does it feel like to focus on the ways He loves and delights in you?

CHAPTER 32

Growing in Faith

"You will seek me and find me when you seek me with
all your heart."
- Jeremiah 29:13 (NIV)

I drive a lot for work these days, and I often encounter construction or closed roads. I've had to learn alternate routes to get where I need to go. Similarly, growing in faith can occur in many different ways. Ways that have worked for you in the past may be just like those closed roads, unable to help you get where you want to go. It doesn't mean they'll be closed forever, but you have to find a new way for now. I used to connect with God by sitting silently, praying in my head, and making space to listen. At some point, instead of feeling connected to God during that time, I started hearing my grocery list and being distracted by the chores I needed to do or a big project coming up at work. I had to let myself be flexible and find other ways to connect with Him when that avenue didn't seem to work. I think the hardest part was the void I felt as I desperately tried to connect with Him but failed to do so.

As I've continued to grow in my faith, using various rhythms and resources, I've noticed one powerful common denominator: a daily pursuit of the Lord. Through my daily time with God, regardless of what that time looks like, God always uses it to build a foundation in me even when it doesn't feel fruitful. This foundational connection with God is where everything in your faith journey begins. Through daily connection, you build your faithfulness and witness God's unwavering commitment to you, aligning your heart to hear God's guidance and make Him the most important part of your life. Whether you set aside three minutes or three hours, every moment spent with God is precious, and God values every second. Though these simple habits may seem small, they have a powerful impact, sparking a deep desire for God's guidance, inner peace, and spiritual freedom. As you come to Jesus genuinely and openly, you'll experience a profound sense of completeness and calm.

That time of connection looks different from day to day and season to season. I adopt new rhythms and stop others depending on what I need and what feels fruitful at the time. It could look like doing a structured devotional each day or reading a chapter of the Bible. It may also look like journaling all my thoughts or participating in an imaginative prayer. The list is endless. I hope that these suggestions feel more freeing than overwhelming, because ultimately, God can connect with us in any activity where we acknowledge Him and invite Him in. What has made the most significant impact on my faith journey is ensuring that regardless of how I choose to engage with God, I do so consistently. This commitment has driven my spiritual growth, allowing me to witness the transformative power of daily devotion to the Lord.

As we pursue God daily, we will notice our lives beginning to reflect His character and values, and that can be embodied in many ways:

- Our interactions with others become saturated with love, compassion, and grace. We become agents of positive change in our communities, offering compassion, encouragement, and a comforting smile to those in need.

- The daily infusion of His wisdom guides us in making decisions that align with His divine plan for our lives, fostering a sense of purpose and fulfillment that transcends our earthly pursuits.

- Our perspective on life's challenges changes. We begin to see difficulties not as insurmountable obstacles but as opportunities for growth and reliance on God's strength. Even in times of sorrow and loss, we find solace in knowing He walks beside us, sharing our grief and providing comfort.

- His unwavering presence becomes a source of resilience, enabling us to navigate life's twists and turns with steadfast faith and hope.

- He is always present with us, but this daily pursuit trains us to be more aware of His presence. Through that awareness, we naturally come to Him more often, not just in those intentional set-aside quiet times, but throughout our days, decisions, and interactions as well.

Spiritual growth is not necessarily our responsibility. Our responsibility is to position ourselves where God can do His transformative work. And when we do, He will.

QUESTIONS TO CONSIDER:

1. How do you currently approach your connection with God, and how consistent is your commitment to it?

2. What are some common challenges or distractions that hinder you from dedicating time to nurture your faith daily?

3. What types of daily faith activities resonate with you the most, and why do you think they hold significance for you?

4. How can you create a more intentional and consistent daily faith routine, and what steps can you take to overcome any obstacles in your path?

ACTIVITY:

CONSTRUCTION ZONE

Use the image below to reflect on ways you've connected with God in the past that don't seem fruitful in this season (the closed road), reflect on familiar ways that are still working as you seek Him and follow His direction, and consider a few new ways to connect with Him that you haven't tried yet. Pick one new thing and try it each day this week. (If you're stumped, think about some of the ideas listed above: imaginative prayer, daily devotional, reading a chapter of the Bible, praying and listening, worship, etc.)

CHAPTER 33

God Prepares Us

*"But now, O Lord, you are our Father; we are the clay, and you
are our potter; we are all the work of your hand."*
- Isaiah 64:8 (ESV)

During the COVID-19 quarantine, a lot of people took up new hobbies. I, on the other hand, used that time to try new recipes. One of them was a copycat Chipotle salad dressing, and it was delicious! I was living with friends, so I made a batch big enough to share. After we ate, my friend was kind enough to put it away for me. The next day, I got it from the fridge and shook it a little to mix it up. What I didn't realize was that my friend did not put it in a spill-proof container, so when I shook it, it went everywhere, and I mean *everywhere*. I stood in the kitchen, toeing the line between laughing hysterically and being thoroughly annoyed at the giant mess I now had to clean up. I laughed and cleaned simultaneously, then texted a friend to share this embarrassing moment that just occurred.

The following day, as I was journaling about how God pours out His blessings, that situation was immediately brought to mind. I thought about how different things need different types of containers. It led to a revelation that in the waiting seasons, God is forming us into the right "container" for what He wants to pour out next. If He would have given me what I now have five years ago, I would never have been prepared for it. I wouldn't have been able to manage it, hold it properly, or steward it well, and He knew that. This is why, in His kindness, He waited to give it to me until I was formed into the right container for what He had for me. We might put things in the wrong containers, but God won't. God won't put anything in you until you're ready, and that means that everything in you is exactly where it is meant to be.

Think of yourself as clay in the hands of God, the Master Sculptor. He gently, yet intentionally, shapes and molds us into the exact right "container" for what He has in store for us—both for what He has created us to give and what He has planned for us to receive. And that could be anything! This life is full of unpredictability in terms of the types of opportunities that come our way and the path our lives will take. But that path is divinely paved for us. So long before we even know what's ahead, God is already shaping us.

Imagine a sculptor at work carefully forming a lump of clay into a bowl, a vase, or a mug. In this process, the sculptor applies pressure in specific areas, removes excess parts, and smooths surfaces. Each touch, though it may seem firm, is done with a purpose: to create a beautiful and functional piece of art.

Similarly, God, in His divine craftsmanship, forms us. Like the clay on the potter's wheel, we may feel the pressure of His hands in our lives, shaping us, removing the unnecessary pieces, and smoothing our rough edges. This isn't always comfortable. Sometimes, it feels challenging, much like how clay endures the sculptor's firm but necessary hand. But this is God's way of preparing us, making us the right vessel for the blessings and responsibilities He has planned. Just as a sculptor visualizes the final form of the clay, God knows exactly what He is shaping us to be, even when we don't. He applies, or allows, just the right amount of pressure at just the right time, in just the right places, ensuring that we are molded into vessels capable of holding His blessings and beautifully crafted to fulfill our unique purpose in His grand design. This builds our character, endurance, and reliance on the potter.

God's preparation of us is both a gentle and a deliberate act, transforming us into exactly what we need to be able to receive and hold the blessings and the work He has in store for us. Remembering this in our seasons of waiting and choosing to reframe them as seasons of preparation could be the key to unlocking a whole new perspective. What if we decided to pay attention to how we are being formed? What if we viewed pressure as formation and cutting off unnecessary pieces as an opportunity for freedom? By embracing the sculptor's purpose in every touch, we open ourselves to the transformative power of His craft, finding beauty and strength in the process of becoming vessels ready to be filled.

QUESTIONS TO CONSIDER:

1. What does the idea of being God's "vessel" mean to you?

2. Can you recall a time when a challenging situation turned out to be a pivotal moment of growth or blessing in your life? Reflect on that.

3. In what ways have you experienced being reshaped or remolded by God, and how did it impact your faith journey? How did it prepare you for what came next?

4. How do the concepts of patience and trust play into our understanding of being molded by God?

ACTIVITY:

In and around the clay, indicate where you feel God's influence and shaping. Using illustrations, words, or any other form, reflect on the shaping that is occurring, your awareness of it, how you feel about it, and how it impacts each area of your life: personally, professionally, spiritually, relationally, etc.

CHAPTER 34

Embracing the Call to Servanthood

"As Jesus and his disciples were on their way, he came to a village where a woman named Martha opened her home to him. She had a sister called Mary, who sat at the Lord's feet listening to what he said. But Martha was distracted by all the preparations that had to be made. She came to him and asked, 'Lord, don't you care that my sister has left me to do the work by myself? Tell her to help me!'"

'Martha, Martha,' the Lord answered, 'you are worried and upset about many things, but few things are needed—or indeed only one. Mary has chosen what is better, and it will not be taken away from her.'"

- Luke 10:38-42 (NIV)

D oes anyone else feel a little more like Martha than Mary? I do, and I used to be so ashamed to admit that because, for so long, my perception of this interaction went something like this:

Jesus is sitting in a chair, and Mary is sitting so close to Him that she may as well be sitting on His feet. The kitchen is to Jesus' left. Martha is working hard in the kitchen and continues to look up at Jesus and Mary as resentment grows in her heart for Mary's laziness and lack of help. Martha finally goes over to Jesus, asking Him to make Mary help her. Jesus, without even looking up at her and continuing to keep eye contact with Mary, says Martha's name harshly twice as if to reprimand her, telling her that Mary chose what's better, and He isn't taking that away from her. When I read that, I imagined Jesus's voice in an angry tone. I felt Jesus not even giving Martha a glance.

That doesn't sound much like the Jesus I've come to know and love, but as someone who for so long related to Martha in this story, there was always a piece of me wondering if God was reprimanding me, too. But I had the story all wrong. I got His character all mixed up. Of course, Jesus saw her–*truly* saw her. He understood Martha's intentions and her heart that wanted to serve Him. He recognized and appreciated her hospitality. Of course, He looked at Martha with His kind eyes and spoke to her with gentleness and love. He wasn't yelling at her, He was inviting her! He was inviting her to rest and to abide. What He wanted more than her hospitality was *her*. He was saying, "There is a time and place for everything, including cleaning and preparing meals, but right now, I'm offering you something better. Take a break. Come sit with me."

What a beautiful invitation that is! It's the one I think we all long for sometimes. Just the one that says it's okay to lay down the weight of life's demands and expectations and just be. Just be with Him and embrace the rest He offers.

The part of this story I kept getting stuck on however, even after all those realizations, was Jesus saying Martha's name twice. I could only compare it to when I was a child and my parents called my name twice, usually in moments when I wasn't listening, and the second time surely was not in a kind or gentle tone.. But after studying this passage, God led me to a revelation that changed everything. In Scripture, using someone's name twice is a sign of intimacy and occurs in instances of invitation an conection. Examples of God calling someone's name twice occur all throughout the bible, including:

- God calling Moses from the burning bush: Exodus 3:4 (NIV), "When the Lord saw that he had gone over to look, God called to him from within the bush, 'Moses! Moses!' And Moses said, 'Here I am.'"

- God Calling Samuel while he was sleeping: 1 Samuel 3:10 (NIV), "The Lord came and stood there, calling as at the other times, 'Samuel! Samuel!' Then Samuel said, 'Speak, for your servant is listening.'"

- Jesus even called the name of His Father twice while on the cross: Matthew 27:46 (NIV), "About three in the afternoon Jesus cried out in a loud voice, 'Eli, Eli, lema sabachthani?' (which means 'My God, my God, why have you forsaken me?')."

These instances are all invitations to come close. They are gentle, kind, and relational. As if that wasn't enough of a perspective shift, God led me to one more place, John 10:3. It says that the good shepherd "calls his own sheep by name" (NIV). So, in saying Martha's name twice, He was speaking belonging over her *twice*.

Serving is valuable, and we are called to it. We get to embrace this opportunity to serve in partnership with God. But that kind of service can only start at Jesus's feet. It is the result of an overflow of what we have received from Him and is an opportunity to give Him an offering. So it's not that Martha was doing anything wrong, just maybe in the wrong order.

The story of Martha and Mary is a profound reminder of the delicate balance between service and communion. As followers of Christ, we are called to embrace the call to servanthood, to offer our efforts and hospitality in His name. However, this narrative teaches us that the essence of true servitude begins not in the flurry of activities but in the quiet moments at Jesus' feet, absorbing His words and presence. Martha's experience is not a rebuke but a gentle invitation to reorder her priorities, placing her relationship with Christ at the forefront. We are given that same invitation. In this space of intimate communion, we are filled, renewed, and equipped to serve effectively. Through our time with Him, we learn to discern the how, when, why, and what of servanthood. This story is not just about choosing the "better part," but understanding that our service is most fruitful when it flows from a heart deeply connected with Jesus.

As we navigate the demands of life, may we continually seek these moments of stillness with Him, for in His presence, we find the strength, guidance, and love necessary to serve with joy and purpose. Let us then step forward, carrying both the heart of Martha's hospitality and Mary's devotion, embodying the true essence of servanthood in our daily walk with Christ.

QUESTIONS TO CONSIDER:

1. In what ways do you relate to Martha? To Mary?

2. In what situations have you felt torn between "doing" and "being," and how did you resolve, confront, or navigate this conflict?

3. What practical steps can we take to incorporate the lessons from Martha and Mary's story into our daily practice of faith and servanthood?

4. What lessons can we learn from Jesus' interaction with Martha about the power of words to convey love and belonging?

ACTIVITY:

VENN DIAGRAM

In the Venn Diagram below, write and reflect on the characteristics needed in that area and how you embody them or want to. In the overlapping section, write down aspects that integrate service and worship, reflecting on how both are essential in your spiritual life.

Martha's Service

Mary's Worship

CHAPTER 35

Sabbath

"Then he said to them, 'The Sabbath was made for the sake of people, and not people for the Sabbath.'"
- Mark 2:27 (TPT)

Doesn't it feel nice to be invited to rest? To nap? Take a break? Go on a vacation? Or simply cease work of any kind? Taking a weekly sabbath can be a difficult rhythm to start, yet it's an invitation we are offered every single week. Our culture keeps us moving faster and forward. It feeds us the lie that if we slow down, pause, or stop entirely, even if just for a day, we are somehow falling behind, missing out, or won't have time to do all the things we need to do. That's not true. That is the way of the world, but that is not the way of God's kingdom.

God models Sabbath rest for us in Genesis when He rested after six days of creating. Learning to trust that God would be able to do more with my six days than I could do in seven was an active discipline for a while. I had to remind myself to follow God's way and not the world's... but now it's second nature. Week after week, He shows me He's faithful!

It hasn't always been easy, though. At times, I've become so rigid on my sabbath "rules" that it became more about following them than engaging with God and allowing Him to fill me up. But that was never His intention. Sabbath is not an opportunity for God to place more rules on me, like a burden to carry. Instead, it's an opportunity for us to find joy. If you're anything like me and get stuck in rule following and aren't feeling much delight, I encourage you to remember that the Sabbath is a gift and to find rhythms that work for you. For some people, cooking feels like work. If that's you, take a break from cooking. For me, cooking brings out my creativity, wakes up my taste buds, and excites me, so I often cook during Sabbath.

As we delve deeper into the essence of Sabbath, we uncover a profound truth: it's not merely a pause in our weekly routine, but a deliberate invitation to participate in God's divine dance of work and rest. Resting on Sabbath goes so far beyond sleeping, instead tapping into these places within us and around us that make us come alive. It is through embracing this sacred rhythm, we align ourselves with the very heartbeat of His kingdom. What a generous God we have that He sets aside an entire day each week simply for our delight and restoration! Just as God demonstrated in Genesis, our Creator intimately understands the necessity of rest woven into the fabric of existence. It's an acknowledgment that our value is not determined by ceaseless productivity but by the loving intention behind our creation. So, let us not succumb to the world's pace but rather dance to the rhythm of grace, finding fulfillment in the cadence of His design. In the sacred hush of Sabbath, we discover that God's faithful provision exceeds our striving, and in surrendering to this divine dance, we find a joy that transcends the world's limitations.

Find what works for you and embrace the freedom that it can look different each week. Sabbath is a gift that we get to unwrap over and over again. Open your heart, eyes, hands, and calendar, and prepare to receive.

QUESTIONS TO CONSIDER:

1. Why do you think God makes Sabbath a command rather than a suggestion?

2. What are activities that bring you TRUE rest? List them.

3. Sabbath can be by yourself, with others, or a mix of both. Do the activities you listed fall in one category more than the other? If so, what is that saying to you?

4. How does engaging in Sabbath rest impact your relationship with God? What about your relationship with others?

5. What are other "fruits" produced through the Sabbath? How do you know if your Sabbath is contributing to fruitfulness?

ACTIVITY:

Pick one joyful, restful activity from your list in Question 2 and do it! Put it on the calendar and do it. Then, reflect on what that activity felt like and how it impacted the rest of your day/week/interactions, etc.

CHAPTER 36

Be

"I am standing in absolute stillness, silent before the one I love,
waiting as long as it takes for him to rescue me. Only God is my
Savior, and he will not fail me."
- Psalm 62:5 (TPT)

For most of my life I've taught kids, and teaching has taught me that not every activity is about the final product. As adults, we often operate with the final product as our goal and don't tend to choose activities that don't have a purpose. I think that's why adults stop playing. It seems childish because it seems to have no purpose.

In childcare and education, there are two main kinds of activities. Project-based activities focus on the final product, and process-based activities focus on children engaging in the process, regardless of the final product. There aren't rubrics, goals, expectations, or rules. Project-based activities look like when preschoolers do cute art activities during the holidays–a reindeer made out of hand prints, a Christmas tree made from popsicle sticks, or an ornament to put on the tree. Those activities aim for the child to produce that product as closely as possible to the teacher's model. On the other hand, a process art activity would be a painting activity simply for the fun of painting, sensory exploration, and creativity. Ultimately, each kid ends up with something, but there is no mold it is supposed to fit, no grade, rubric, or specific end goal. Everyone's will look different, and everyone's will be great! The "goal" is to participate.I wonder if we mislabel activities in our lives. Our culture has a project-oriented mindset, where everything is focused with outcomes, driven by goals, and shaped into products. We constantly evaluate whether what we are doing is good enough or valuable enough. We compare, and we use these arbitrary rules to try to make sense of where we and the things we do fit in the hierarchy. I'm curious if there may be process activities in my life that I'm mislabeling and treating as product activities. I wonder what it would look like if we gave ourselves that permission. What if the process WAS the goal? What if it isn't how well we do something or how we do it, but just that we are doing it at all?

It should be easy to just "be," but it can feel so unnatural, can't it? I want you to picture a lazy river. You know the one I'm talking about–it's the most relaxing activity at a water park. All you do is hop in a raft and float down a man-made river. By no effort of your own, you circle the entire waterpark, getting to see it from all angles. You're completely still and moving forward simultaneously. It's easy to assume "being" means not moving, but like the lazy river, that's not how it works when God is involved.

There is a long list of things that make "being" hard for me. If there's something I'm praying about and waiting on, I want it to come faster. I want to know what to do to speed up the process. If dishes are in the sink or an unread text on my phone, it requires a lot of self-control to leave those dishes undone and the text unread. If I have a rough day at work, my mind spins, so I mentally relive my day instead of being where I am physically. By trial and error, I've learned some techniques: listening to music, leaving my phone in another room or on silent, intentionally praying over my day, and choosing to move my body, which all help to ground me in moments when I'm distracted. These practices allow me to wait well when I'd rather speed to the end. I ask God questions and invite Him into the moments ahead of me: "What do you have for me here, God?" "What ways do I need refreshed today?" "Which areas of my life need rejuvenated?"

Coming to the Lord daily in that same sense of stillness, with a heart posture of invitation, is critical if we want to hear Him. If we invite Him, He will be present, and He will speak. Sometimes, His answer isn't immediate, but it always comes.

What would it be like if today was the beginning of us collectively choosing to rest, be, listen, and focus on the process rather than the destination? I think it would look like a lot of people hearing the gentle whispers of the Lord and falling in love with a Father who provides every single time.

QUESTIONS TO CONSIDER:

1. Why is it hard to just "be"?

2. In what area are you finding it most challenging? Is there something you're waiting on? Is it your ability to stay in the moment during your day?

3. What are the most common things that try to pull you out of that state of rest and stillness?

4. What are practical steps you can take to remove these distractions or fight those urges to "do more," "be more," "work more," "hurry up," etc.?

   Pay attention to those things today and see if you notice any precursors or red flags alerting you that your attention is being pulled away from where you want it to be.

ACTIVITY:

Pick a mindful activity. I use activity lightly because this isn't about producing or doing. For some, that may look like a walk by yourself, free from music, your phone, and other distractions. For others, it may be yoga or biking, painting or cooking, or even sitting in silence. Pick something that is more of a process activity than a product activity, where you can be intentional about being present where your feet are and present with God.

SECTION 3

Launch

This section of the book focuses on knowing where we are being sent and the gifts within us that we need to nurture (or allow to be nurtured) to go where He is sending.

CHAPTER 37

Launch

> *"Then I heard the Lord asking, 'Whom should I send as a messenger to this people? Who will go for us?' I said, 'Here I am. Send me.'"*
> *- Isaiah 6:8 (NLT)*

Something shifts when we believe that God wants to send us. From that belief, we develop a willingness to be sent.

I was excited when God gave me the word "launch" as my word of the year for 2022. It means to hurl forward with intensity. It was as if all that work of releasing and unleashing led to this year—this moment: the opportunity to be launched wherever God wanted me, and believe me, I was ready (or so I thought). I felt like I had spent so much time doing that hard work of releasing, and then during the year of unleashing, I constantly felt like the runner at the starting line, waiting for the buzzer to sound so I could take off. I felt equipped, but I waited for God to give me the green light. Giving me the word "launch" felt like that green light I was waiting for. It became clear that this was not just about a single moment of action, but a continuous process of aligning with God's will. This alignment requires a deep understanding of our strengths, weaknesses, passions, and fears. It's about knowing who we are in Christ and how our unique design fits into God's greater plan.

When the word "launch" began resonating in my heart, I understood it as a call to action. This is the time to put into practice all that I have learned about myself and about God. To break down what that could look like, I used the letters of the word launch to describe myself- both the person I am and the person I'm becoming. These are the things I wanted to continue embodying as I walked forward into whatever God was calling me to.

Loving

Authentic

Understanding

Nurturing

Child of God

Hopeful

His call for me was to move forward with boldness and faith, trusting that God has equipped me for the work He has set before me. I had to keep myself rooted in who He says I am because my identity keeps me steady. That doesn't change even when my situation does. I realized that my years of releasing and unleashing were healing me, freeing me, and clearing out distractions so I could see the path forward. Now I am hopping in the catapult and saying "yes" to wherever He launches me. At the beginning of my year of launching, I continued seeking God on what He wanted to launch me into. Writing, sharing my faith, being open about my emotions, and even new relationships blossomed from my "yes." The thing about a word of the year is that it's another filter, so to speak, that we can run things through to see if we are on the right track. If an opportunity comes my way, I can hold it up to the word launch, and I can ask God, "does this align?"

This doesn't mean that the path will be easy or that I have all the answers. I definitely don't. It's much more about this confidence God built within me that He would be there guiding my steps. It involves being attentive to the Holy Spirit's leading, being willing to take risks, and being open to God's redirection when necessary.

This call to being launched could easily have been rephrased as a call to be brave and to take steps outside of myself. So much of the previous few years of work was internal and underground–completely unseen. But now it felt like things were beginning to bloom above ground. As those things bloom, it is vital to remain rooted in God's Word and a community of believers. Such grounding provided wisdom, encouragement, and discernment as I navigated new challenges and opportunities. It also offered a space for accountability and growth, ensuring that I stay aligned with God's will and not my own ambitions. As I embarked on this journey of being "launched" into God's work, I prayed that I would do so wholeheartedly, with a heart that seeks to glorify Him in all things.

It is a journey of stepping into the unknown with the assurance that God is leading the way. This is the essence of being launched–it's about embracing the adventure that God has in store, using every lesson learned, every moment of growth, and every bit of strength He has provided to fulfill His glorious purpose.

QUESTIONS TO CONSIDER:

1. Reflect on a time when you felt like you were waiting for God's "green light." How did you discern His timing and direction?

2. What are some things you are praying and hoping God will launch you into?

3. What do you think God wants to build in you before launching you into something new?

4. How do you identify and nurture the strengths, talents, and passions God has given you to fulfill His purpose?

ACTIVITY:

On the puzzle to the left, write, draw, or display gifts, skills, talents, personality traits, etc, that God has instilled in you that encompass who you are. These things can guide you in discerning who, where, and how you were created to display His character and be His hands and feet.

On the puzzle to the right, write, draw, or display characteristics of God that resonate most with you and how you relate to Him. Consider this completed illustration a tangible reminder of why He is trustworthy: to hold your dreams in His hands and to direct your heart and steps.

CHAPTER 38

Jehovah-Jireh - My Provider

"Look at the birds. They don't plant or harvest or store food in barns, for your heavenly Father feeds them. And aren't you far more valuable to him than they are?"
- Matthew 6:26 (NLT)

O ur culture is designed for striving for all the things we want and need. This results in many of us being overworked, overtired, overly available, under pressure, under-rested, and fueled by comparison. There is a misconception that we must do it all, be it all, produce it all, and do so out of our own strength. Results, results, results. But God tells a vastly different story, and choosing to make decisions based on God's way is a holy act of rebellion.

God loves to provide for us abundantly and consistently, and His provision is a through line in the Bible. When the Israelites were in the desert, God provided for them. Manna fell from the sky every day for them to eat, but they were only allowed to take what they needed for that specific day, forcing them to rely on Him to provide again the next day. There was no hoarding or storing up in barns. There was no planting or harvesting, taking control, or ensuring they had food "just in case" God didn't come through. They relied on God daily, and He proved His faithfulness.

The way many of our lives are set up, our striving to provide for ourselves prevents us from full reliance on God. We have the ability to save money, we have a pantry full of food, and we have the resources to buy the things we need and want. In that, it can be easy to lose sight of who our actual provider is. It's common to get stuck thinking that when God says He will provide for us, He only refers to material things. What He's promising is to provide for ALL of our needs. Comfort, strength, rest, peace, ideas, patience, direction, love, finances, joy, food, purpose, community, healing, connection, and so much more.

The realities of God's provision became very real to me in 2020. The housing market was wildly unpredictable and fiercely competitive, but I was searching for a home. The living situation I had at the time changed, and I ended up searching non-stop for an apartment on very short notice. There were four weeks between leaving the place I was living and the apartment that I was preparing to move into when I essentially didn't have a home. What I did have were incredible friends. I don't think it was an accident that three different families had back to back week-long vacations where they coincidentally needed a "house sitter." They were incredibly kind and allowed me to live there while they were out of town. Another family had a comfy couch I was able to stay on and they showed up to help me on moving day. I spent a few nights in that apartment before officially moving in, so, on my first few nights, I didn't even have a bed. Again, my people showed up for me. A friend literally drove a futon mattress through the neighborhood so I'd have something to sleep on. While yes, those were physical needs that were met, my emotional needs were also met: safety, security, comfort, rest, and the joy and connection that comes with accepting and receiving help from people who love me.

I give that story to show that God's provision is sometimes miraculous, unexplainable, and clearly supernatural. Other times, probably more often than not, His provision comes through people. Whether through the supernatural or through humanity, His provision is no less divine. We get to participate in that too, so when we feel God's prompting to pick up the tab at breakfast or offer our assistance in some way, ask yourself, "What if He is providing for them through me?"

I've found that in my own life, I've been most anxious when I wasn't sure God really meant He'd provide for all of my needs. The anxiety I was feeling pointed to doubts I had about whether God really would do what He said He'd do. As I continue walking with Him, He builds a richer history of being my provider. So, each day, it gets a little easier to say "God's got this." He cares about every detail of your life, and if He provides for the birds, He surely will provide for you.

QUESTIONS TO CONSIDER:

1. In what areas do you successfully surrender and trust His provision?

   - What do you notice about yourself when you rely entirely on God?

2. Do you ever find yourself accidentally taking credit for the things God has provided for you?

3. Is there an area where you struggle to trust His provision?

   - What do you notice about yourself when you are not entirely reliant on God?

4. What step can you take towards surrendering one of those areas of struggle and stepping into total reliance on Him?

ACTIVITY:

JOURNALS

- Skim through your current and previous journals, looking for God's provision.

- Create a list of ways God has provided for you.

- Specifically, note anything that did not seem like provision at the time but became apparent after the fact.

1. How does it feel to see those things in writing?

2. Does that change your perspective on anything happening right now?

CHAPTER 39

Direction and Discernment

"I will instruct you and teach you in the way you should go;
I will counsel you [who are willing to learn] with My eye upon
you."
- Psalm 32:8 (AMP)

I am a chaser of beauty: sunrises, sunsets, rainbows, you name it. Thousands of pictures of the sky occupy my phone's photo album. I'm always looking for the big, beautiful, undeniable signs of our Creator, still doing His intricate creative work.

I remember one day I was driving on a dark, muggy day. The clouds were gray and gross. Nothing to take pictures of, that's for sure. But then I felt so clearly in my spirit God say to me, "I made this, too." It occurred to me that unless it was big, beautiful, colorful, and clear, I disregarded it. I realized that in trying to experience God, hear from Him, or understand where He was leading, I was looking for big, undeniable signs. But God pointed to something so much more ordinary to remind me that His presence is visible there, too.

I have this same faulty mindset regarding big decisions. I struggle and drag my feet because I'm waiting for God to clearly indicate which decision is the right one. I don't want to get a new job, start a business, or go on an expensive international trip unless I know it's in alignment with Him. But the thing is, I don't always get the clear sign I'm looking for, and sometimes, while I wait for the sign that isn't coming, I miss out on something I should have said "yes" to or experience something I should have said "no" to.

God promises to guide and instruct us, but it isn't always in the form of these undeniable signs. Sometimes, I only look for the billboard with flashing lights that says, "Go this way," but God is speaking in a whisper, and I miss it. Even when those billboards don't show up, God has given us tools of discernment that we have access to right now.

He has given you your body, access to Himself through prayer, and His Word in the Bible. And hopefully, there is at least one person in your life who speaks truth as a wise counselor for you. He has also instilled passions, gifts, and interests within you, and as you ponder the ways those things equip you, it may help point you toward the right path.

This next part took me a long time to wrap my head around, but hear me out: there may also be decisions you face where there is no right or wrong choice, and the decision truly is yours. Of course God cares about our decisions, but He gives us the freedom to choose. The key in discerning these situations for me has been to get to the root of God's actual call. Is He leading me to buy a house so I can set down roots in this city (which can be done through many different houses), or is He calling me to a specific house? Is God calling me to a job where I can spread light and encouragement and joy (which can be done in many occupations), or is He calling me to a specific job? I have to look more closely at the "why" before I decide on the "where" or "how." Something else I do in that process is to pray for God to give me peace in the right decision, and disturb my peace if I'm walking the wrong way. I ask Him to open the door to an opportunity so wide I can't miss it, and to shut all the other doors so tightly that even if I wanted to, I wouldn't be able to get through. It's a practice of inviting Him to move in whatever way He wants, and giving ourselves the space to pay attention to our thoughts, our feelings, our bodily responses, instruction from scripture, and wise counsel from those around us.

Sometimes God does give big signs, and I love it when He does! But when He doesn't, remember that He isn't leaving you hanging. Instead, He is allowing you the space to access the tools He has already given you, empowering you to do the brave and challenging work of discernment.

QUESTIONS TO CONSIDER:

1. When you need to say "yes" or "no" to something, where do you feel that in your body?

2. How can prayer help you discern the right decision to make?

3. How can you run your decisions through the lens of the Bible to determine if they align with who God is and what He wants for you?

4. When looking back at times of decision, how have you experienced God's presence?

   - Are you more focused on doing the right thing, or who you are becoming in the process?

ACTIVITY:

Think about a decision you must make where you wish you knew what God wanted you to do.

- Make a list of what excites and scares you about taking a step in that area.

- What do your gifts and passions say about that decision?

- How are you feeling in your body as you approach this decision?

- Do you think this decision has a straightforward "right" or "wrong"? Or is this a decision where God may not have an opinion on the outcome?

- Have you shared this decision with a trusted friend? (Consider doing that this week, if not.) What is that friend saying to you about that decision?

- What does the Bible say that can guide you in this decision?

Set aside time today to pray and journal about this area of your life. What is God saying to you? What patterns are you noticing? Take a hard look at the fears you listed. Is God asking you to keep waiting or say no, or is it the enemy planting fears that stop you from saying "yes" and pursuing what God wants for you?

CHAPTER 40

Discovering my Purpose

"I admit that I haven't yet acquired the absolute fullness that
I'm pursuing, but I run with passion into his abundance so that
I may reach the purpose for which Jesus Christ laid hold of me to
make me his own."
- Philippians 3:12 (TPT)

s a kid, I loved playing capture the flag! It required some fast running, dodging obstacles and people in my way, and a team working toward a common goal. I wouldn't even notice how exhausting that game was until the next day when my body would be sore, because in the moment, there was an all-encompassing joy that overshadowed everything else. Since then, the only times I run now are with kids. It seems to be one of their favorite activities. Why is it that they love to run? They love the chase and the wind in their faces. There is giggling and a childlike joy that is worth noting, and I have an urge to capture it.

As an adult, I don't enjoy running. But when I see Philippians 3:12, I try to conjure up the childlike joy I felt playing capture the flag. God is clear what we are running towards. We are running to Him and whatever purpose He has outlined for us. The key is there *is* a purpose. There will be distractions and obstacles we will have to face along the way, but we will also get to laugh and feel the wind on our faces and feel the joy. Not just in the fulfillment, but in the running too.

Running toward the purpose God has for us is different for each person. I might be running towards God in my writing, while you are running towards God as you faithfully serve your family. Someone else may be running towards international mission work while someone else is building a business. Our purpose above all is to run towards Him, seek Him, and not just run our ideas past Him, but let the ideas come from Him! Purpose is such a big concept, so I want to make sure to be clear: we may have different purposes in different seasons, but can honor God in all of it.

Before any of us can run, we must figure out which direction to go. The gracious thing about God is that He isn't hiding that information from us. He wants us to discover it! Discover, as defined by the Collins Dictionary, is an active word meaning to find after searching.[4] There is action on our part, an uncovering of sorts. I often wish God would tell me something unmistakably clearly, but I think there are reasons He doesn't do that often, especially when it comes to something big, like purpose. There is beauty in the process of discovering.

---

4 "Discover," Collins English Dictionary, HarperCollins, accessed January 31, 2024, www.collinsdictionary.com/dictionary/english/discover.

Think about archeologists who discover ancient temples buried underground for thousands of years. They don't find the whole temple at once. They first see a piece. They have no clue what it is, but it fuels excitement and curiosity, so they continue to dig, and little by little, this massive structure is uncovered. But they must keep bringing their tools and showing up at the same spot every day, even though they don't know what they will find. They have to put in the time and energy to dig deep. It's not all that different in our faith. To uncover our purpose, we must show up to that space with God daily. We have to dig deep with Him, and little by little, piece by piece, He speaks our purpose over us and gives us everything we need to run towards the fulfillment of it.

God is freeing you up to run after something! And everything He's shown you about who you are and how He created you are tools in your tool belt. He wouldn't give you a hammer if you weren't going to hit nails, or maybe pull out some nails. He wouldn't give you a shovel if you weren't going to be digging. There are things about you that He gave you because they are necessary tools for your purpose in this season. Pay attention to what tools you have available and ask Him why. Just as a hammer has multiple uses, our gifts, passions, and skills do, too. Bring those tools to Him and let Him speak over you today, and let us each respond with the courage to pick up our tools and follow Him.

Questions to Consider:

1. If you had to pick one emotion you feel as you read Philippians 3:12 (TPT), what emotion would that be?

    *   Why do you think that verse feels _____ (insert above emotion) for you?

2. How can you seek and discover your God-given purpose, aligning your passions and gifts with His calling for your life?

3. Think about some of the "tools" He has given you through your giftings, character, resources, personality, etc. How can those things clarify what He has revealed about your purpose so far?

4. How can you discern what God wants you to pursue versus what you want to pursue?

ACTIVITY:

DIGGING

Take a look at this image. Imagine you are the person digging to discover something new. What are the tools that God has given you? Label them. Then, write anything and everything you know about what God is calling you to do in this season. If you don't know anything yet, pray about it and how to dig deeper to discover it.

CHAPTER 41

Obedience

"Jesus replied, 'Loving me empowers you to obey my word. And my Father will love you so deeply that we will come to you and make you our dwelling place.'"
- John 14:23 (TPT)

I've been on countless family vacations, and many of them go like this: the GPS says to get off the exit, but my dad thinks he knows the way, so he chooses to go straight. He didn't realize that there was construction straight ahead that had traffic backed up for 40 minutes or more. He wanted to go the way he thought he knew, but it took him into trouble that he didn't foresee.

We can have a flawed perception of obedience when we don't truly understand it. Obedience isn't a way that God keeps us enslaved; it's the pathway toward freedom, joy, and abundant life. Sometimes, God may ask you to do big things like sell your house, pursue a new career, invite someone to move in with you, apologize to someone, etc. But His call isn't always that big. He gives us daily opportunities to be obedient, like when you feel you should reach out to a specific friend, send someone a card in the mail, take a meal to a neighbor, encourage your coworker, or take a Sabbath. I'm sure you're already thinking of things He's asked you to do. In those moments, the Holy Spirit is on the move. Those nudges aren't coincidental.

Or, maybe it's not so much the "what," but the "when" or the "how." God knows the roadblocks up ahead. He also knows what we need to build within us to be equipped for where He is taking us, and often, the journey is what equips us. He may not always lead us on a trouble-free path, but we can trust Him as our guide because He knows and sees things up ahead that we cannot. The best part is that the more time we spend with Him, the more our love for Him empowers our "yes" to everything He asks us to do. Our history with Him proves that our obedience is for our good and leads to all the beautiful things He has planned for us. God knows the path to abundant life, and it is often paved with His directions and our "yes."

Thankfully, He is also a God who is patient and kind. When we choose to go our own way, He is our faithful GPS, rerouting us back to His path. There is nothing we can do to thwart His plan. We may delay it a bit, but as we repent and continue turning back to Him, He will always reroute us back to Himself.

Obedience can be hard. One of the hardest things God has asked me to do was to quit a job I loved with absolutely no idea of where to go next. I did quit, and gave a few months' notice, out of respect for a team and a program I cared deeply about. I stressed for most of those months, wondering if I made a mistake, wondering if I heard God correctly, over and over again having to confirm to those around me that I was confident in my decision, when in reality I wasn't. I wasn't confident in my decision, but I was confident that God would help me figure it out. He did.

One of the most encouraging things in that season was this comparison to a father and daughter. If I believe my dad is asking something of me, and I respond accordingly, he isn't going to be mad that I heard him incorrectly. He will be proud that I thought I heard something from him and I followed. God is the same way. He delights in our attempts to follow His lead. Even if we are wrong, if our heart is in the posture of obedience, He is proud nonetheless. And His protection isn't just for our "correct" decisions, but for every single moment, every single decision, and every part of our lives. Even if we are wrong, His protection is still there.   Many of us don't like to be told what to do. If we fully trust God's direction, sometimes familiarity hinders our "yes." If we think we know a better or more comfortable way forward, we may not choose God's way. God's way is often paved with unknowns, but anything unknown to us is known to God, and I'd rather follow Him into the unknown than follow myself somewhere comfortable and familiar. I want to approach opportunities for obedience out of my love for Him, knowing that there are unknowns along His path that are far beyond anything I could ever ask, think, or imagine, and I want that. I want that with Him!

1. Do you trust that God's desires for you are good? What motivates you to listen for His voice and obey?

2. How have your motivations changed as you have gotten closer to Jesus?

3. Where in your life are you being disobedient or delaying your obedience?

4. What is one way you've been obedient to God recently? What does it look like to obey God more recklessly today?

Take a moment to pray and ask God what He has next for you. Once you hear from Him, write it down. What is one step you can take towards being obedient in that area? What will it cost to take that step?

MAKE A LIST

Reference the sheet of paper below:

- On the left side, list some things God has asked you to do recently. Do you notice any patterns about the items themselves or how he spoke them to you?

- For the things you obeyed, who/what helped you be obedient?

- On the right side, write the result of being obedient in those moments. If you weren't obedient, take some time to reflect on that. What do you think God was trying to do in those moments?

- For the things you did not obey: what was your hesitation? What prevented your obedience?

Take a moment to pray and ask God what He has next for you. Once you hear from Him, write it down. What is one step you can take towards being obedient in that area? What will it cost to take that step?

CHAPTER 42

God Equips the Called

> *"Then Moses said to the Lord, 'Please, Lord, I am not a man of words (eloquent, fluent), neither before nor since You have spoken to Your servant; for I am slow of speech and tongue.' The Lord said to him, 'Who has made man's mouth? Or who makes the mute or the deaf, or the seeing or the blind? Is it not I, the Lord? Now then go, and I, even I, will be with your mouth, and will teach you what you shall say.'"*
> *- Exodus 4:10-12 (AMP)*

I don't know about you, but it makes me feel much better when I see people in the Bible like Moses feeling ill-equipped for the work God is calling them to do. I feel like that a lot. I often need reminders like this one to be re-centered in the truth that God will never call us to do something He won't equip us for. He will never send us a place where He isn't going with us.

I work in an early intervention program for kids who have Autism. The most meaningful part of the job for me is the process of helping kids who are non-verbal learn how to speak. In the thirty-one years I've been on this planet, I've never witnessed miracles and experienced God quite the way I have in the midst of this process. In addition to God clearly showing up for each of these amazing little kids, He's shown up in significant ways for me, too.

It's vulnerable to try something new. Each of these kids has had to learn to use their voice in a new way. Trying to make a specific sound is hard for them, yet they keep trying and bravely use their voice in a way they never have before. Whether they make the sound correctly or not, they keep trying. They trust me as I gently guide them. They are brave! Through this experience, God showed me that in the same way that I am guiding these kids to bravely show up and learn to use their voice, He was calling me to do the same through my writing. I felt ill-equipped, but what a disservice to my kids if I wasn't willing to enter into the same level of vulnerability and bravery I am asking of them. If I truly believed He would equip them, why did I not have that same level of belief that He could equip me?

For me, learning to use my voice looks like writing words in a journal and sharing them with you. For them, it's learning to use their words verbally to communicate with those around them. It may not always come out the right way, but they keep trying and showing up. As they learned to use their voice, I learned to use mine, too. It takes patience, perseverance, and practice. *Lots* of practice. And I think the way that I approach our kids is the way God approaches me. He is my gentle guide, my patient teacher, and the one cheering me on as I practice and persevere. He gives me all the tools

I need. He is ever present and ever on my side. He doesn't get upset with me that I'm not perfect. He's calling me out in a new way, and He'll teach me everything I need to know. God is the one doing the work in our kids and in me. He might use worldly means to do it, but the miracle and the masterpiece are His!

I don't know what He is calling you to do, but I know He equips, guides, and delights in your attempts. Whatever it is, that thing you've felt nudged towards, but it scares you? What if you walked toward it instead of away from it? He isn't calling us to be perfect. He asks us to say "yes" and bravely walk with Him, trusting Him to equip us thoroughly for all He calls us to do.

QUESTIONS TO CONSIDER:

1. Jot down your initial thoughts about this verse and the reflection. What is God bringing to your mind? Maybe take a few minutes in silence to see if God has anything specific to say.

2. What is something you currently feel ill-equipped for?
   - What aspects of it specifically are shaking your confidence?

3. As you reflect on that, are you noticing any things God has placed in your life, such as people, experiences, gifts, character traits, etc., to help equip you?
   - Are you embracing and welcoming those things?

4. What would it look like to approach new challenges with a baseline knowledge that you are equipped and that God is walking with you?

ACTIVITY:

TOOL BOX

On the tools listed below, write some of the tools you believe God has already equipped you with as a visual reminder that you have all that you need.

Then on the toolbox, rewrite this verse as if it were written about you. What is He asking of you? What is your hesitation? How do you think He would respond? Then end it with a quick prayer trusting Him to equip you.

CHAPTER 43

Devotion

"Your spiritual roots go deeply into his life as you are continually infused with strength, encouraged in every way. For you are established in the faith you have absorbed and enriched by your devotion to him!"
- Colossians 2:7 (TPT)

God often speaks to me through very tangible analogies and I absolutely love it. I think He knows that I need it. Somehow, He takes spiritual concepts and abstract ideas and makes them really practical for me. I love how I can eat a pizza roll and see a lesson on patience, look at the sky and see God's infinite creativity, and spill salad dressing on the floor and feel God illustrating a lesson on capacity. He is so kind to not just tell me, but show me.

This morning was no different. I was on a walk and saw an electrical tower. I've walked that road hundreds of times, but typically the trees, thick with leaves, fill the open space and cover most of this tower. I never paid any attention to it before. Today I felt captivated by it. It's massive and sturdy, and it occurred to me that this tower was the singular thing powering so much of my neighborhood. The tower was standing tall on a power grid and holding up electrical wires that take power to homes and businesses around my city. I immediately thought about what a perfect illustration this is for how God works. Those power lines are powerless if they aren't connected to the power grid. They are not the *source* of power, but the avenue through which that power moves.

Similarly, when we are connected to God, His power is active within us. And not *just* power, but our connection to Him is the avenue through which we are infused with strength, invigorated with courage, and blessed with all that a truly abundant life encompasses. What flows from Him into us doesn't just bless us; it touches everyone we come into contact with. When we are connected to Him, everything we touch has the opportunity to be touched by Him. As I look more closely at Colossians 2:7, the phrase "Enriched by your devotion to him" catches my eye. Devotion is profound dedication; consecration; earnest attachment to a cause, person, etc., an assignment or appropriation to any purpose, cause, etc. (dictionary.com) It is our earnest attachment to Him that enriches us in all the ways He promises.

We must nurture this relationship and be aware of warning signs that arise when our connection weakens. When we are connected to Wifi on our computer, an alert will pop up to tell us when that signal is weak. When that happens, we often move closer to the router or the source. Similarly, signs in our lives alert us when our connection to the Lord is weak, and moving closer to God always helps. The signals we get when this weakened connection happens may differ, but the answer is always the same. Move closer to God. Lean in. Adjust your spiritual antenna.

A few signs I experience when my connection with God is weaker are changes in my language, insecurity, comparison rising in me, questions surrounding my identity and whether I am loved, and constant distractions. When I notice those signals popping up, I intentionally shift to prioritize God. He wants to infuse you with Himself and all His presence offers, and the avenue to do that is through a well-nurtured connection with Him. Then, when you are filled, that same power, strength, joy, hope, and wisdom you experience in your relationship with the Lord begins to overflow.

QUESTIONS TO CONSIDER:

1. What does it look like to devote yourself to the Lord?

2. How would you rate your current connection with God?

3. In what ways are you currently prioritizing and nurturing your relationship with Him?

4. Throughout your whole time knowing and loving Jesus, what has been your favorite way to nurture your relationship with Him?

ACTIVITY:

SIGNAL VERIFICATION

On the Power Low" alert, write, draw, or use symbols to indicate your answers to the following:

1. What signs do you notice in your heart, mind, and body that alert you that your connection is weak?

2. What intentional shifts can you make to lean into Him when you notice those signals?

   On the power grid, write, draw, or use symbols to indicate your answers to the following:

3. What are some things God pours into you through your connection with Him?

4. What are some things He is pouring out through you into the people, places, and spaces you interact with regularly?

5. How does it feel to know that connection with Him is always readily available to you?

CHAPTER 44

Overcoming Obstacles and Opposition

"I have told you these things, so that in me you may have peace.
In this world you will have trouble. But take heart! I have
overcome the world."
- John 16:33 (NIV)

What if getting a concussion was a gift of grace?

It seems like a silly question to consider after months of struggles, speech therapy, and trying desperately to remember details from conversations. In the game of "is this a gift or not?" it is easy to write this one off with a big fat "no." But looking deeper, I see how God consistently uses even my difficulties for good. This concussion was no exception. What could easily hold me back taught me to overcome. What could have isolated me actually deepened my relationships. What could quickly force me backward into old self-deprecating ways has propelled me forward into self-compassion.

Here are a few things God taught me through this concussion...

Concussions have a wide variety of symptoms that can occur at varying levels of severity. Once the initial physical symptoms subsided, I mostly struggled with heightened emotional states, forgetfulness, inattentiveness, and confusion. In many ways, these symptoms challenged me. I had to get used to asking questions and often admit forgetting something important. It became more apparent in this season that I used to feel like I had it all together. My schedule was managed, I remembered everything I needed to remember, and I had it under control. One of the problems with living that way is that it isolates you. It doesn't require you to need anyone else. Sometimes, it tricks us into thinking we don't need God either, and that's a dangerous place to be. We are wired to need each other and designed to be held up, not by our own strength, but by God's, as vulnerable as that is. It's not a weakness to need others. It's Biblical, and we all become stronger through connections with one another. The effort I put into having it all together before was a level of striving I was so desensitized to that I didn't even see it. Now that I'm free from it, I feel a weight lifted, a weight I didn't know I was carrying. This loss made me feel weak at first, but now I feel free. This freedom is a gift I couldn't see before, but I see it now.

I've always felt like one of my strengths, and something I offer this world, is my ability to thoughtfully remember things about the people I love. If they have a prayer request or a birthday, if they're going on a trip somewhere or have a first date, if they like a new snack they found at the store, or share something with me that they are learning, I want to be able to talk to them about it. I want to pray for them, ask how things are going, find out about their date, or maybe pick up their new favorite snack as a surprise on a random Tuesday. I felt like this quality is core to who I am. It's how I'm wired and show up for the people around me. It never occurred to me how those things all hinged upon me having a good memory. I felt like I lost a massive piece of who I am when I lost that. I had to figure out who I was and how to still show up thoughtfully and honestly with others, whether that piece of me was working correctly or not.

I learned that people love me because of who I am, not because I can do everything listed above. I began to watch as those qualities of thoughtfulness and generosity played out in new ways. It's not that my core identity changed, but instead, those characteristics were playing out in a new way. As one of my friends generously reminded me, we never really lose pieces of who we are. In some seasons certain parts of us take center stage, and other parts take a more supporting role, or even a role backstage. Those characteristics core to who we are are never truly lost. That's a reminder I needed. It was a shift at first, but now I can see that a concussion, what I thought would hinder me, actually expanded my capacity. It showed me new ways to show up as wholly me.

I wouldn't have chosen a concussion, but I no longer wish it away. I see the gifts in the here and now and grab hold of them, trying not to let a single one slip through my fingers. It's like Christmas morning–I spend time sitting with each gift, learning about it and how to use it, before moving on to open and appreciate the next. I'm sure there are more gifts here that I have yet to uncover. The difference is that when it first occurred, all I could see was how this situation sucked. Now, my perspective is that of a treasure hunter with eyes primed to see the treasure. Perspective changes everything. I see the gifts.

I'm unsure what you're facing, but I encourage you to evaluate your perspective. Even in the situations that wreck us in every way, God promises to use them for good. That doesn't erase the bad or invalidate your feelings about it. Please hear me on that. God invites us to bring our grief, sadness, confusion, and pain straight to Him. God using it for good allows us to hold joy and pain together. Grief and hope. Opposing things at the same time. All of it is welcome at the same time. Where is the good? Where is the gift? Dig around for it. Uncover it. Ask the Lord to reveal it. Hold it like the precious treasure it is, and don't let it go. What if the gift He brings in the middle of dark moments is the one that lights a whole new path forward?

As I continue this vital identity work, I recognize that the work may never be finished. There will likely always be situations that challenge my convictions about who I am, and it's precisely through that challenge that my convictions can be strengthened and that lies I've been unknowingly believing about myself can be brought into the light. Our wholeness can be strangled by the lies unknowingly woven through the threads of our identity. Bringing them into the light may feel like being broken, but it's really the beginning of being made whole.

QUESTIONS TO CONSIDER:

1. Can you think of a challenging experience in your life that, in hindsight, you now see as a gift or a valuable lesson? How did your perspective on that experience change over time?

2. The devotion emphasizes the importance of vulnerability, relying on others, and embracing change. How can you apply these ideas of embracing vulnerability, relying on others, and viewing obstacles as opportunities when navigating adversity?

3. How can you actively seek out and appreciate the positive aspects or lessons in challenging circumstances you may currently be facing?

4. How might your sense of identity be strengthened or transformed through the challenges you've encountered or are currently experiencing?

ACTIVITY:

AFFIRMATION

Create a short (1-2 sentence) affirmation statement that you can refer to and speak over yourself in the midst of difficulties. Post it somewhere where you can see it daily.

CHAPTER 45

Making All Things New

> *"And God-Enthroned spoke to me and said, 'Consider this! I am making everything to be new and fresh. Write down at once all that I have told you, because each word is trustworthy and dependable.'"*
> *- Revelation 21:5 (TPT)*

I bought an old, partially broken kitchen hutch online for $25 a few years ago and decided to turn it into a wine cabinet. I had never taken on a furniture project before and was excited about it. I underestimated the difficulty involved in restoring furniture, so I let it sit in the basement for weeks, only touching it here and there. That is, until I started grieving. Grief propelled me into creativity–a creativity that God used to heal me.

I was blindsided by grief, and it sent me into one of my lowest places. I had been acquainted with grief prior to this moment, but this grief felt different. In the past, I have experienced the loss of loved ones. Death is undeniably tragic; it feels final. Yet, we are also filled with hope because eternity awaits us, and reunions are certain. Experiencing the loss of a relationship was different–totally new territory. The person wasn't gone. He was still out there, living his own life, but a life separate from me. It was a grief that overtook me because I wasn't just grieving the person and his presence, but also the future that I envisioned for myself. It feels final, but only to an extent, because he is still out there. I didn't know how to process that.

Figuratively in my heart and literally into my basement, I walked into a low place. Day by day, scraping paint by hand, sanding, priming, painting, and drilling. It started as a way to put my idle hands to work and use my body to work through things I was thinking or feeling. Each day, this project gave me something to look forward to. It gave me a vision to work towards and a creative outlet for all my pent-up energy and emotion. When I got home from work each day, I changed into my grungy clothes and returned to the basement. I didn't realize initially that God was using this project to heal me, one brush stroke at a time, making me new.

As I was dealing with the death of something in my heart, I was bringing to life something new with my hands. The cabinet continued taking shape as hours turned into weeks of hard work. As the wine cabinet came together, pieces of me were coming back together, too. I was becoming whole again.

One of the most profound moments during this project was as I was sanding and scraping all of the old paint off. I realized that to make it new, there was a stripping process that had to occur. Removal of something so engrained, connected, and stuck had to occur before it could be covered with something new. I realized what was playing out right in front of my eyes was happening in my heart. Something was being stripped away so I could be covered in His newness.

The cabinet is finished now. It's black with gray wood accents, a backsplash, lighting, a towel holder, a wine rack, and a mini fridge. Whenever I look at the cabinet, which is now proudly displayed in my dining area, I think about how God used it to heal me. While I was making something new, He was making *me* new. He placed a desire in my heart and the ad for the cabinet on my newsfeed, preparing me for a season I didn't know I was entering. This project was ready for me when I needed it most. It is a piece of my healing journey and a tangible reminder that God is still in the healing business.

God loves to redeem and restore us! Piece by piece, He makes us new. We may not always realize it in the moment, but I bet if you look back, there are lost puzzle pieces of your life that Jesus connected: weak places that He strengthened, old mindsets He has replaced with new ones, lies He has freed you from that have been displaced by truth. Maybe even a struggle you endured that brought you a little closer to Him and helped you become a little more *you*. No matter how stuck we feel, how broken, or how weighed down by grief, always remember that our God is making all things new.

QUESTIONS TO CONSIDER:

1. Why does Revelation 21:5 use the words "new" and "fresh"? How are they different, and why is that significant to His promise?

2. Where in your life have you noticed God's restorative hand?

3. What things would you like God to make "new and fresh"?

   • What signs may you notice when God is working that way?

4. What does writing down everything (the second half of this verse) have to do with God making all things new (the first half of the verse)?

ACTIVITY:

MAKING ME NEW

God continues making us new. There is no limit to how He will refine us to be more accurate representations of Him and more authentic versions of ourselves. Categorize different seasons of your life on the paint cans below. You can label them with years or a color you would use to describe that season. My season of grief would have been "2022: Quick Sand Brown."

On the paint scraper what is God stripping away or asking you to let go of for Him to make you new?

Sanding Block- what situations has God used to transform you?

CHAPTER 46

Embracing God's Guidance

"Joyful are those you discipline, Lord, those you teach with your instructions."
- Psalm 94:12 (NLT)

I don't like to be corrected. It often fills me with shame and anxiety. Sometimes, it even taps into my feelings of worthlessness. But God deals with us differently than the boss we struggle to take feedback from or the parent who is unfairly harsh. Multiple times in the Bible, it says God's discipline and correction are gifts that bring joy. Psalm 119 goes as far as to say that the psalmist delights in His commandments and there are wonderful truths in His instruction.

It's such a natural response for us to recoil when we are corrected. Still, we are reminded that when God corrects us as His children,

He acknowledges and speaks our identity over us every single time. He corrects us because we are His sons and daughters, and He loves us deeply. His correction is for our benefit, and His guidance and instruction are the clearest way forward. So, how do we let His correction and guidance bring us joy?

We need to start by looking at what joy is. Joy in these verses is the Hebrew word "Chara."[5] It means joy, delight, and a source of gladness. It has the root word "xar," which refers to recognizing God's grace and displays this idea of having joy because of grace. I love this so much because it is out of His grace that He corrects us. It's an overflow of His love that says, "Come this way," "Try this," "Your current ways are hurting you," and "Follow my lead." He's not criticizing us. He wants the best for us.

I haven't always heard His correction in the tender voice of a father. It sounded more like anger, like the moments just before being whacked with a wooden spoon. But that isn't who God is. His guidance, correction, and instruction show me the way I should go. They are available to you, too! He is kind and compassionate, not forcing us to follow His ways. But He offers us direction so that the signs are there if we want to go His way. It's important to remember that His guidance doesn't always come in the form of correction. Sometimes, it also comes in the form of affirmation, letting us know we are on the right track! We have to keep our eyes peeled for those messages, too.

Following God's lead and yielding to His correction is for His greatest glory and our greatest good. I rarely know for certain what I'm supposed to be doing or where my life is headed. As I seek Him,

5 Strong, *Strong's Concordance*, 5479.

He shows me the way, in the big things and the daily seemingly mundane things. Where He leads me always produces more fruit than anything I could do on my own. One gift of His correction and guidance is that they are fully drenched in His grace. He isn't mad at us when we go the wrong way, or make a decision that we thought would be best but ended up hurting us more than it helped. He just wants to show us a new and better way. He wants wholeness for us. He wants fullness for us. He wants closeness with us. He wants *us*!

He doesn't want us showing up as counterfeit versions of someone else. He wants us to fully embody the masterpiece He created us to be and be fully available and equipped to run towards His work and receive His promises for us there. God gets the most glory when we allow ourselves to see through His eyes, appreciating ourselves as unique expressions of His love and character. Every day, we get to show Him we agree with Him and that who He created us to be is better than anything we could try to manifest on our own. Unless we become humble receivers of the correction He offers, we will never cross the threshold of His promises.

QUESTIONS TO CONSIDER:

1. Have you ever experienced God's guidance or correction? If so, how has He shown that to you? What did it feel like?

2. How does it impact your perspective to know that His correction points you in the direction of all the promises He has for you?

3. What are you currently asking God for His guidance on? Are you hearing Him respond?

4. Have you experienced moments of joy while guided and instructed by Him? What might lead you to experience more of His joy in those moments?

ACTIVITY:

LIGHTHOUSE

- By the Lighthouse's light, write about any clear ways God has directed you back to His path when you were off track. Near the buoys, write about the affirmations you've received that you were on his path.

- In the water, write about any joy you experienced in the process of God's guidance and correction.

- On the shoreline, write about the joy you've received once you've arrived at where God was leading you.

CHAPTER 47

Walking in God's Timing

"When YAHWEH delights in how you live your life, he
establishes your every step."
- Psalm 37:23 (TPT)

We all experience times in life when it feels like we are merely surviving—putting one foot in front of the other each day, yet going nowhere. Each morning, we wake up feeling as if we are in the same place we were the day before. During one particular season, I found myself asking God what the point of it all was. I felt exhausted and stuck, despite my efforts to move forward.

I remember one of those seasons of my life so vividly. Standing in my kitchen, I texted a friend, asking for prayers for endurance. I'll never forget what she said to me. She described my journey with God like a long staircase. She encouraged me by saying that each step

I took was still a step forward, even though it felt like I wasn't getting closer to the top–to what I felt called to do in that season, to God, to community, or any of the other things that were on my heart. My feelings weren't a true representation of the staircase.

I didn't feel like I was on a staircase though. I *felt* like I was on a Stairmaster, where the same four steps were repeated over and over. I was moving, but simultaneously felt stationary. The effort was great, yet the progress seemed non-existent.

Here's the thing: God never forces us to follow Him. It's a choice made out of love for a God who deeply loved us first. Our choice to follow, and our obedient steps are a response to Who He is and His invitation to be close to Him. Each day, we get the choice to take another step forward up the stairway towards Him or to take a step off, effectively giving up.

If we falsely believe that our effort is wasted on a Stairmaster-like faith, we could step off, and that's that. But we're not on a Stairmaster, we are on a staircase, inching toward God with each step we make. Hypothetically, what if we choose to stop taking steps? To quit picking up one foot after the other? I'd encourage you to consider that we don't know when the fruit of our faith will bloom. What if we are on step ninety-nine of one-hundred and stop one step short of our goal? Chances are we probably wouldn't know how close we came to the reality of our desire, the deepening of our faith, or whatever it is we're partnering with Him on.

The point is, what if we are so close and have no idea? Could we choose to live like that? To live as if we believe that today could be the last step we take before we step into what's next? As we step into our dream? Our purpose? The good works He prepared for us in advance? What if we are one step away? How would that change how you live today?

For me, it changed everything. I'm not saying that realization immediately gave me a burst of energy or instilled this reserve of perseverance to draw from. Still, it did renew my belief that perseverance is worth it. Our consistency and diligent pursuit of the Lord is always rewarded, but it will likely also be hard. In fact, if you're anything like me, I actually trip up the stairs more than I trip down them. Our stumbling does not mean we have to tumble back to the beginning. Let Him catch you, pick you up, dust you off, and cheer you on towards Him.

God isn't taking us on a journey for the sake of perseverance alone. Our perseverance builds things in us that prepare us for what's next. We don't necessarily know when "next" will come, but we can hold onto hope that there is a next and that God, the Author of time, is waiting for the exact right moment.

This theme has continued to rise up over the years. I'd get discouraged whenever I hit a new waiting season that felt too long for me. I knew I needed a way to permanently mark and remember God's faithfulness, perfect timing, and ability to use my perseverance for something good. So, in January 2023, I got the Greek word "Hupomone" tattooed on my arm. Its meaning encompasses steadfastness, consistency, active endurance, and sustaining perseverance. It's about being active rather than passive in trials and waiting seasons; our endurance in those moments produces good fruit. The design of my tattoo has the word running through the middle of a mountain range. I chose mountains because my life and faith journey are full of peaks and valleys. I wanted the word to run right through the middle because it's in the middle ground, the "not yet" parts of life, where my active endurance meets God's faithfulness. Every. Single. Time.

God's timing is something we can't understand on this side of Heaven. What we can do is trust the One who controls the timeline and, with active perseverance, continue climbing the staircase closer to Him until He whispers those sweet words, "You've made it."

Questions to Consider:

1. What areas of your life aren't following the timeline you hoped they would?

2. What do you think God is trying to build in you as you wait?

3. What ways can you pursue active endurance?

4. Reflect on a time when God's timing wasn't making sense, but in hindsight, He came through for you at the exact right time.

Activity:

STAIRMASTER VS STAIRCASE FAITH

Write down on the Stairmaster areas where you feel your efforts aren't yielding progress.

On the staircase, write down areas of your life where you can tell you're moving forward.

Reflect on what it would look like if you stepped off one step too soon.

What if you knew today would be the last day before reaching that goal, dream, or desire you're walking toward? How would that change the way you live today?

CHAPTER 48

Embracing a Lifestyle of Worship

"Therefore, I urge you brothers and sisters, in view of God's mercy, to offer your bodies as a living sacrifice, holy and pleasing to God—this is your true and proper worship."
- Romans 12:1 (NIV)

Growing up I didn't really care much about my body, and I certainly didn't care *for* it. I didn't view myself as God's masterpiece. Instead, I figured I could make up for my own body image struggles by being the helpful one or the nice one and by embracing opportunities for self-deprecating humor. What I continue to learn as I get older is that there's a better way. How we treat our bodies matters. Not just to improve our self confidence, but actually so that we can use our body to worship God and serve those around us. You've probably heard a lot recently about a whole slew of things you can do to take care of your body in our current self-care culture. I'm definitely an advocate for self-care (check my planner for my upcoming facials), but the self-care in Romans 12:1 encompasses much more.

Of course, God wants our bodies to be nourished with good foods and movement so we stay healthy and strong. Of course, God wants us to treat our bodies kindly, look at ourselves with compassion, and set ourselves apart as if our bodies are holy–because they are. God perfected our bodies, and His spirit dwells within us. So what we do with them matters.

How can we worship God with our bodies? Well, I think an excellent way to figure that out is by going through the various parts of your body and thinking about how you can use them for God. Ask yourself: What are my hands working on? Who are my hands helping or hugging? What kind of content am I letting my eyes see? What am I noticing, and what am I doing about what I'm noticing? What am I eating? What kind of words am I speaking? What songs am I singing? Who am I encouraging?

And before you let this become a set of rules you have to follow or let this verse push you into a health and wellness journey, I'd encourage you to consider how choosing to have an ice cream cone also worships God. He created things for us to enjoy and delight in. Adding that pumpkin spice creamer to your coffee in October, enjoying that giant sugary lemonade from the lemonade stand down the street during mid-July heat, eating an extra s'more with your family over the campfire, or going to a happy hour after work to celebrate a successful week ... God delights in each of these things, and they can be worship, too! The flavors, the community, the memories, all those things matter to God. We don't need to earn treats, and God surely isn't anti-treat either. When you're laughing with people you love as ice cream drips off the cone and all over your hand, take a moment to remember that it is worship, and thank the Lord for His kindness.

The key is balance. God wants to use our hands to help others *and* to care for ourselves. God wants us to eat nourishing foods, *and* He loves when we enjoy a treat. God wants us to speak kindly to others *and* speak kindly to ourselves. It's all about the *and*.

Our bodies are beautifully complex, and with that, there are many ways we can use our bodies to worship God. Those ways can even differ from person to person. If you make music, make it. If creating art makes your soul come alive, choose to do that. Like to cook? Share your food with people. Our bodies aren't always used for things that delight in and worship God, but we get the opportunity to make that choice. Our bodies are involved in everything we do, so everything we do *can* be worship. Choose to worship.

QUESTIONS TO CONSIDER:

1. What does worship feel like?

2. What is your favorite way to worship God?

3. Is there anything you do to prepare your heart for worship or to get in a posture of pouring out to Him in that way?

4. How can you create more moments of intentional worship throughout your day?

5. Is there a specific characteristic of God that consistently turns your heart towards worship? What is it? And why do you think that particular thing stirs your heart for Him so profoundly?

ACTIVITY:

WORSHIP WITH MY LIFE

Within the thought bubbles, write or draw some of the things that move your heart toward worship.

Next to each part of the body, write the ways you use that part of the body to worship God.

CHAPTER 49

Running Your Unique Race

> *"Therefore, since we are surrounded by such a huge crowd of witnesses to the life of faith, let us strip off every weight that slows us down, especially the sin that so easily trips us up. And let us run with endurance the race that God has set before us."*
> *- Hebrews 12:1 (NLT)*

O ur true identity is one of our greatest gifts; however, for many of us, overcoming the false identities to embrace our true selves is our biggest challenge.

The race that God has set before us is predetermined, and we have been divinely equipped to run that race. Knowing who God is and who He created us to be is the starting point of our destiny. If we don't know who we are or how He uniquely equipped us with specific gifts, skills, and passions, how will we know we are on the right path? I can think of plenty of times in my own life when I've watched someone else running their race and wanted to run that race, too. Whatever that race was, I would see the success, money, connection, comfort, or recognition people got from doing their own things, and those would seem like very attractive paths to walk in my own life. The problem is, I either wasn't equipped or created to do those things, or it wasn't the right timing. I spent a lot of my twenties looking at what other people were doing and deciding I wanted that too-watching people around me working straight to the top of the corporate ladder, becoming entrepreneurs, quitting their jobs to follow their passions, getting married young, and having kids ... all of these things captured my attention, stole my focus, and tempted me to try walking someone else's path instead of finding my own. Comparison is a thief, and whether I knew it or not, I was being robbed.

I realized early on that I have a passion for working with kids. They bring me so much joy and prompt a silly, more lighthearted side of me to emerge. As someone who spends so much of their life as a deep thinker and deep feeler, I love and cherish those lighter pieces of me! I very quickly realized that God had a race for me to run that involved serving and loving the kids He put in my path. In embracing my unique race, I had to let go of some of the things I was watching others do. I wasn't going to make a ton of money or work my way up some organizational ladder. I had the opportunity to loosen my grip on what I thought I wanted so I could instead fall in love with the life God laid right before me.

The call for me to serve kids has looked a lot of different ways over the last fifteen years: working at a camp and in a school, a clinic, and in the community, and even becoming more active in the lives of my friends' kids. In each setting, I continue to evaluate if I feel like I'm still using my gifts the way God wants me to, or if I need to make a shift. As hard as it has been, I've made a few shifts. In each new avenue of using my gifts to serve kids, I always see God's goodness there. I feel at home when I'm in my lane. Sure, imposter syndrome comes along every once in a while, trying to convince me that I don't belong. But the difference is, when I'm in my lane, imposter syndrome can be overcome by confidence in my identity. When I'm trying to run someone else's race, it's more than imposter syndrome, I'm an actual imposter.

Our race isn't really a smooth run, though I wish it were. I picture it more like hurdle-jumping on a track. Before the horn even blows to begin the race, I need to line up in the right lane. Then, even when I'm in the right lane, obstacles still come my way, and I have the opportunity to overcome them. Each one, shaping my character to be more like God and building more of the qualities within me that will allow me to finish this race, confidently and fruitfully.

In our lives, the boundaries of our path are laid out for us through our identity. In life, we are offered thousands of opportunities and millions of choices and are constantly being pulled in different directions. We need to know the skills, gifts, and qualities God has blessed us with. In each season of life, those questions around our core identity can help us to know which lane to start in, and which lane to stay in. Let's pay attention to the things that fill our hearts with joy, compassion, and empathy and move us into action. Each of those seemingly simple things about us plays a part in our design and purpose. If we don't know what those things are, we will never learn how to use them for His kingdom.

The best part is that God promises to go with you. He's next to you and behind you. He's gone before you, and lives within you. As you run towards whatever He is calling you to today, you will learn more about Him, yourself, and the eternal significance of what He is doing through you. Keep saying "yes," even when it's hard. Keep enduring. Keep seeking Him and His heart. You won't regret it.

QUESTIONS TO CONSIDER:

1. How have you been distracted, tempted, or caught in comparison as you've watched other people run their race?

2. What are some of the gifts, skills, passions, and qualities you have been given and offer this world? If you don't know, consider praying about it, asking God to reveal what He sees in you, and then asking a few trusted friends what they see from an outside perspective.

3. Do you know what the next step on your path is?

4. How is God illuminating your next step?

ACTIVITY:

RUNNING YOUR RACE

Take some time to reflect on this verse using the image below. Pick your lane in the image below, write or draw what you think your next step is.

In the other runners' lanes, write or draw the things that tempt you to fix your eyes on what they are doing and compare rather than keep your eyes fixed ahead of you on God.

Consider what, if anything, is hindering you from running your race fully.

CHAPTER 50

Your Brave "Yes"

> *"The LORD came and stood there, calling as at the other times,*
> *'Samuel! Samuel!' Then Samuel said, 'Speak, for your servant is*
> *listening.'"*
> *- 1 Samuel 3:10 (NIV)*

Every "yes" to God is brave.

My history with God has a long pattern of Him asking me to do hard things. The way He calls us to live, love, and lead is not easy. But big rewards come with our "yesses." Jesus says a mustard seed of faith can move mountains. I've never seen a physical mountain be moved, although I believe God could do that. What I have seen instead, in completely undeniable ways, are mountains moved in people's families, barriers brought down in relationships, generational curses broken, and new stories of truth beginning where people were stuck believing lies. I've seen healing and hope and deliverance and freedom. Sometimes, when we say "yes" to God, we are the recipient of those things, and sometimes, we are the avenue for God to provide those things for someone else.

A couple months ago, a few close friends and I were praying consistently for my Grandma who had been dealing with repeated failed surgeries for a broken arm. One of my friends texted me one morning asking if I had ever prayed with my hands on her arm before. I said that I hadn't, and she responded by saying how that is what she pictured as she was praying for my Grandma. There are a few people in my life, this friend being one of them, who know Jesus and love Him and who know my heart and love me, too. We've been doing life together for years, and I trust her to speak into my life. She prays fiercely, discerns intently, and is full of wisdom and wise counsel. As we talked about her prayer and the vision that she saw, I mentioned that I would be visiting my Grandma that weekend and I felt moved by God to pray over my Grandma just as my friend envisioned.

Leading up to visiting my Grandma, I was feeling incredibly nervous. I don't have a lot of experience praying out loud, and while I grew up in a faith-filled family, their faith was often more private. We all pray for each other, but I had never actually heard anyone pray for each other aloud. I was worried she might think it was weird to lay my hands on her, or that my prayer would be me just nervously stumbling over words, but I continued to pray for courage, if that was what God was leading me to do.

When I arrived for my visit, my sister and Grandpap were also there. I really didn't want to pray for her in front of them. I tried to think of creative solutions to get out of it. My best idea was to tack it on to the mealtime prayer, but that felt more like a cop out than a divine encounter. So, sitting on their living room floor, I prayed for God to make a way. Soon after, my Grandpap left the room. My sister followed. That left just my Grandma in the recliner and myself on the floor below.

Again I prayed for courage, and then I asked her how she had been feeling. She talked about her arm a little, then said, "Look at this part right here," and then continued on by asking me to touch it. God was really handing me this opportunity on a silver platter if I could be brave enough to take it. Hesitantly, I asked if I could pray for her and she was sweetly surprised and excitedly agreed. After I said "Amen" something truly unexpected happened. She began praying for me. It was one of the sweetest moments we've ever shared. I'm not sure if that prayer participated in her healing or if it was just simply for those shared moments with the Father, but it felt like a gift. Something that I thought was only for her, God used to bless us both.

When we step out in faith, saying "yes" to God, it requires us to let go of our need for control and perfection as the Spirit leads us into the unknown. I had to let go of my fear of being weird or saying the wrong things or stumbling over my words entirely. But it was God who paved the way from my "yes" to His miracle. Bravery doesn't mean being unafraid. It just means to move despite being afraid. As we surrender to the rhythm of God's love, we discover that even in the midst of challenges, His grace is a sustaining force. He is there, guiding each step.

In the quiet surrender of our hearts and the bold steps forward, let us continue embracing the adventure that unfolds. He delights in each step taken in faithful response to His call. He might call you to something like writing a book. He also might call you to buy someone a meal, reach out to a friend, wake up early to read your Bible, or to pray out loud for someone. I have no idea what God is calling you to do; those are just a handful of the things He has called me to do. The list is endless. Whatever it is, I can promise you that it's for your good and for His glory. The more we practice following, the easier it gets. I don't mean that the tasks He calls us to require any less courage; rather, it's that His voice becomes clearer, making it easier to hear and trust. As a result, we find ourselves second-guessing His guidance less and embracing the next step with greater confidence.

In 1 Samuel 3:10, Samuel hears God's voice and responds as an eager servant of the Lord. That mattered. How we respond matters, too. Choosing to follow God takes guts, plain and simple. It's a bold move in a world that often pushes us to focus on ourselves and play it safe. It's like deciding to go against the crowd, trusting that the uncharted territory we enter into with Him is better than where we could ever go on our own. People might call it unconventional, but in God's eyes, it's us showing we're up for something bigger. The rewards of this bravery go beyond what you can touch or see right away. It's not about racking up stuff; it's about a heart makeover, getting closer to God, and living a life that fits into an eternal plan.

Saying "yes" to God isn't just answering a call; it's like finding the key to a life filled to the brim with love and grace. It's the kind of journey where bravery isn't just a reaction, but a ticket to a life soaked in the good stuff that God's throwing our way.

QUESTIONS TO CONSIDER:

1. When God calls you to do something, what do you consider before you decide if you'll answer His call?

2. What emotions do you experience when God asks you to do something? How does that impact the speed with which you respond and the response you choose?

3. What is God calling you to do right now? Write about it in as much detail as you currently know.

4. If you were to say "yes" to God's call in question 3, what ways could that impact you? What are you excited you or someone else could gain? What are you afraid you might lose?

   * If you aren't sure what God is calling you to do right now, pray about it. It might not be anything you deem as "big," but anything God calls you to do matters, and it is a brave choice to say "yes"!

ACTIVITY:

MOVING MOUNTAINS

Think about one thing God is calling you to do. Write down and illustrate the mountains that could be moved either for you or someone else by your step of faith and outline any obstacles or fears you may need to overcome to say "yes."

CHAPTER 51

Bearing Fruit for God's Kingdom

"I am the vine; you are the branches. If you remain in me and I in you, you will bear much fruit; apart from me you can do nothing."
- John 15:5 (NIV)

As we walk through the journey of faith, one of the most compelling images Jesus gives us is found in John 15:5. He speaks of Himself as the vine and us as the branches. This simple yet profound metaphor holds deep truths about our relationship with God and our role in bearing fruit for His kingdom. Knowing our role is essential because our energy can be wasted in trying to do God's job instead of our own.

Picture a vineyard. The vine is the source of life for the branches; it provides the nutrients and water they need to grow and bear fruit. The branches are not self-sufficient; their health, growth, and fruitfulness depend entirely on their connection to the vine. This is the picture Jesus paints of our relationship with Him, which is good news!

In the Bible, fruit often symbolizes the outward expression of our inner spiritual condition–things like love, joy, peace, patience, kindness, goodness, faithfulness, gentleness, and self-control (Galatians 5:22-23). These are not just admirable qualities. They are the evidence of Christ's life and power at work within us. Sometimes, we get this idea of fruitfulness misconstrued. It's easy to think that if things are going well and flourishing, it's a sign of fruitfulness, and maybe it is. But a lack of visible fruit and the sense that things aren't thriving does not necessarily indicate a lack of fruitfulness. Often, if we are connected to God, the lack of visible fruit is actually a sign of the work God is doing under the surface. Just like plants, to grow upward and outward, we must first grow deep roots. The root work can't be seen, measured, or quantified, but it's happening, and it's the most important part! Every time I seem to veer off path, feel lost, or overwhelmed, I go back to my roots. I look back on my relationship with God, the things He has taught me and I feel more at home.

Our roots are often built through a continuous showing up, and being open handed for whatever God has for us. Recently, the place I've been showing up with God is my kitchen table. I have been reading Bri McCoy's book *Come & Eat*,[6] which talks about how holy it is to make a place for yourself at your own table. She continues on about the beauty and meaning associated with mealtimes.

---

6 Bri McKoy, *Come and Eat: A Celebration of Love and Grace Around the Everyday Table* (Thomas Nelson, 2017).

I was really wrestling with what it could look like to be intentional about mealtimes in my singleness. I literally said to God, "It just doesn't feel as holy when I show up to the table alone," and immediately, I felt like I heard, "Maybe it's even more holy."

I don't think that it's *more* holy to eat by yourself than to be in community with others, sharing meals and conversation together. It feels easier though (at least for me) to actually sit around the table with others and listen to them and take that time because it matters, and they matter. But when I heard this message from God, I felt this emphasis on the extra effort it takes to show up to a table when the only one who matters in that moment is me.

This prompted me to start showing up at my table during mealtimes. I'll eat on a real plate and without the TV or distractions, and I stop and pray in acknowledgment that food is a gift and this time is set apart. Then as I eat, I've been listening to the "Let's Read the Gospels" Podcast.[7] It's countercultural to turn off the TV, put down my phone, and just be. Day after day, meal after meal, I continue showing up, and I leave feeling full—not just in my stomach, but in my heart. I'm realizing the roots God is building in me are both connecting me to Him but also showing me that in order for others to belong at my table, I have to belong there first.

In a world that often values independence and self-reliance and fills our minds with distractions, this call to remain in Jesus can seem counterintuitive. But there's great freedom in acknowledging our need for Him. It means we don't have to strive in our own strength; we can rest in His. When we face challenges, we can draw on His

---

7 *Let's Read the Gospels.* Hosted by Katie Luse. Kate Luse LLC, 2022–present. Podcast, https://www.katieluse.com/podcast.

wisdom and power. When we feel weak, we can lean on His strength.

Bearing fruit is a process. Just like in nature, spiritual growth and fruitfulness take time. There will be seasons of pruning and times of challenge and refining that may seem painful but are ultimately designed to make us more fruitful (John 15:2). These are the times to cling even more closely to Jesus, trusting in His loving care and purpose.

The invitation is clear, and the promise is sure. Remain in Jesus, and you will bear much fruit. It's not about your ability; it's about your connectivity to Him. In Him, and through Him, you are equipped and empowered to make a lasting impact for God's kingdom. What a privilege and a joy it is to be branches connected to the true Vine!

Questions to Consider:

1. What specific practices or habits help you to remain in Jesus and nurture your spiritual growth?

2. Can you recall a time when you felt disconnected from Jesus? How did it affect your ability to bear fruit?

3. What fruit are you currently seeing in your life?

4. How do you ensure you stay connected to Jesus, the true Vine, in your daily life?

ACTIVITY:

CONNECTION TO THE VINE

On the Left: Create a visual representation of your current connection to Jesus

On the Right: Create a visual representation of your ideal relationship with Jesus

If writing feels easier than drawing, that's okay! Do whatever feels authentic to you.

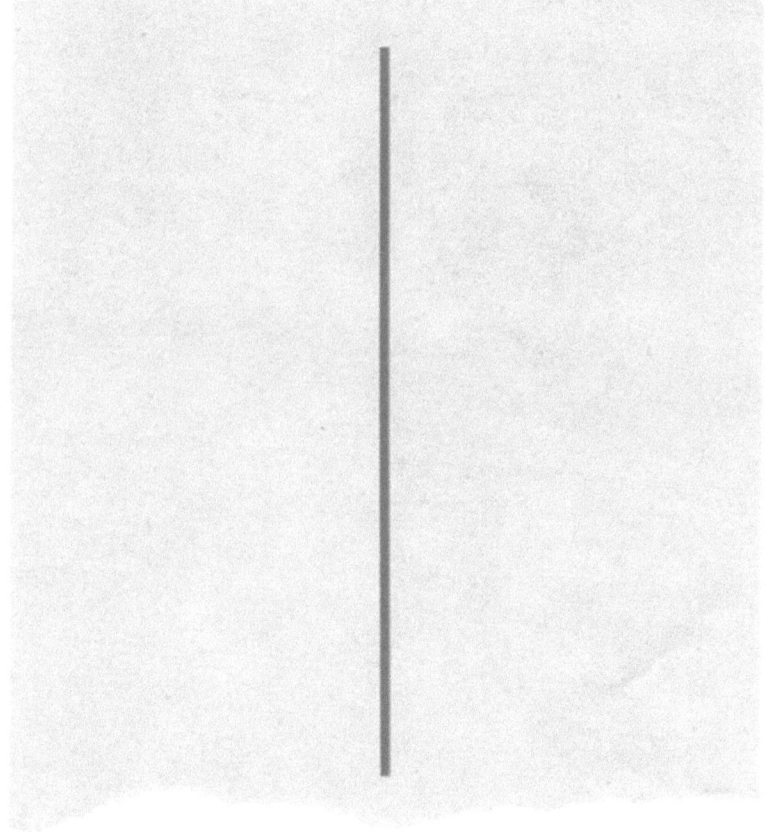

CHAPTER 52

Sustaining the Fruit

"So neither he who plants nor he who waters is anything, but only God who gives the growth. He who plants and he who waters are one, and each will receive his wages according to his labor."
- 1 Corinthians 3:7-8 (ESV)

I don't know about you, but I put a lot of pressure on myself. I set goals and I am constantly measuring myself. I don't do it on purpose; it almost feels ingrained in me sometimes. There is a voice in my head, a berating one that loves to shame me and show me how I don't measure up. Honestly, it's exhausting. That voice is why I often try so hard to make things happen out of my own strength. I feel like if I can make it happen, I've overcome that voice calling me a failure. The good news is that in 1 Corinthians 3:7-8, God takes responsibility for our growth. We get to do our part, but He does the rest. We have access to His strength and don't have to make things happen on our own. How freeing is that?

A few years ago, I learned about this process called grafting. It's a process used with plants and I found it incredibly fascinating. I first discovered it in the footnote of John 15:5. The verse in The Passion Translation reads like this: "I am the sprouting vine and you're my branches. As you live in union with me as your source, fruitfulness will stream from within you—but when you live separated from me you are powerless." A footnote below this verse translates "life union with me" as "grafted into me."

Grafting is a technique in which you join parts from two or more plants, so they appear to grow as a single plant. The upper part of one plant grows by utilizing the root system of the other plant and essentially feeding off of a stronger foundation. This is exactly what we get to do with God. We make Him our foundation and connect ourselves so closely to Him that He fuels our growth, and we grow in His direction. We are incapable of sustaining what God is building. With God, though, *all things* are possible! But that's the key. With God. In Him. Through Him. And in Him, we will always bear fruit.

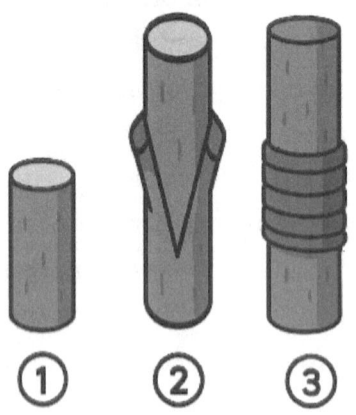

Step 1: Identify a sturdy base, with a deep root system.

Step 2: cut a slit in the middle of the branch and inset another branch into the muddle of it.

Step 3: wrap the branches tightly together so they begin to grow as one

Just as a plant requires constant nurturing—sunlight, water, and nutrients—we, too, need spiritual sustenance to maintain the fruitfulness God cultivates within us. This sustenance comes in various forms: prayer, fellowship, studying the Word, and, importantly, embracing the Holy Spirit's guidance. Each element acts like sunlight or water to our souls, encouraging growth and strengthening our connection with God. Without this continual nurturing, our spiritual growth may falter, just as a plant would wilt without water. Remember, it's not about the intensity of our efforts but the consistency of our surrender to God's nurturing.

In this journey, it's easy to forget that the fruit we bear isn't a badge of our spiritual accomplishment. It's not a trophy on our shelves, screaming of our hard work and dedication. Instead, it's a beautiful, living testament to God's unfailing love and power at work within us. His grace, strength, and life flowing through us produce this fruit. Sometimes, I have to remind myself of this, especially on those days when I feel like I'm just not doing enough or being enough. It's not about striving harder; it's about leaning more into Him, allowing His life to flow through us more fully. It's about resting in the truth that He is the vine, and we are merely the branches, wholly dependent on Him for everything.

And think about this: when a branch bears fruit, it's not hoarding it for itself. The fruit is there to be shared, to provide nourishment and joy to others. In the same way, the fruit that grows in our lives is meant to be shared. It's intended to impact others and show them God's love and character. It's a form of worship—a way of demonstrating God's glory to the world. In those moments when the berating voice in our head starts to whisper lies of inadequacy, let's remember it's not about what we can produce on our own. It's about what God can do through us and how He can use us to touch the lives of others. It's about surrendering to Him and allowing His goodness to flow through us to others. This is the beauty of bearing fruit with God—it's a journey of growth, not just for ourselves but for everyone we encounter along the way.

QUESTIONS TO CONSIDER:

1. In what areas of your life do you put the most pressure on yourself to achieve or succeed? How does this align or conflict with the idea of God being responsible for growth?

2. How does the concept of grafting, with its emphasis on connection and dependence, impact your perspective on your relationship with God?

3. How is God nurturing you? If you don't recognize fruit or His nurturing, reflect on and pray over the fruit you'd like to see and how you currently need to be nurtured. Ask Him for it.

4. Reflecting on the nature metaphors (like the grafting of plants or a branch connected to the vine), how do these images help you understand your spiritual journey? Can you think of any personal experiences that relate to these metaphors?

ACTIVITY:

Engage with this illustration however feels best for you. Consider ways to represent the growth occurring within you and exuding from you. Find ways to represent the things that are nourishing you or draining you. Think about the fruit that God is producing within you and through you. Let Him reveal what He sees, and consider if He may be calling you to shift something to allow yourself to surrender more deeply into union with Him.

CONCLUSION

Closing Thoughts

A much earlier iteration of this journal pulled me close to God during one of my loneliest seasons. He showed up in tangible ways through practical analogies and His overwhelming love. He answered my questions and taught me new things in ways that left breadcrumbs that I wanted to keep following because I couldn't get enough. His Word really is alive! The only One who satisfies me is Him.

I've revisited this journal repeatedly as an opportunity to continue strengthening my roots with Him. I pray that through this journal, He draws you closer, too, and that this journal can become an avenue to continue connecting with Him for many years to come.

With a grateful heart,

Megan

Acknowledgements

I am profoundly grateful for the opportunity to put this book into the world. There were so many people who helped make this possible and who encouraged me as I became the version of myself that was capable of writing this book. That's one of the great gifts of life and of having strong, faith-filled people in your corner– we are always becoming, and the voices of people we invite into our lives help shape who we become. What I once thought was impossible is now a tangible reality. Their contribution to this work and to my life is invaluable. Writing the acknowledgments was one of the hardest parts of this book because over and over, words seemed to fail to express the level of love and gratitude I have towards the people below. If, as you read this, you have people coming to your mind who would be on your life's acknowledgement list, don't wait. Maybe now is the perfect time to tell them what they mean to you.

TO ALL MY MINI BFFS-

I hope that someday you'll get to read this and know that with each page I wrote, I had you in mind. I thought about the things I wish I would have known when I was younger ... things about myself, and things about God. I thought about all the things I hope to embody as your friend. Then, I put it all into this book. Your curiosity and willingness to ask questions inspires me, and it inspires my own willingness to ask curious questions to God. This entire book came from curious questions about topics I didn't totally understand. Being with you reminds me why Jesus calls us to become like children. Sitting with God in my questions produced rich fruit in my relationship with Him and a depth of faith that I didn't know was possible. I pray you continue to embrace your curiosity. I've come to believe it's one of our greatest gifts.

TO MY FAMILY-

Mom and Dad, thank you for making difficult choices that allowed me to be positioned in places that built into my faith. Thank you for encouraging me to prioritize youth group, mission trips, and being an active member of our church growing up. Thank you for showing me what it means to humbly serve others and to use our gifts for His glory. These things shaped me more than I realized. When I became an adult and got to choose for myself Who I follow and what I believe, the foundation laid beneath me was a sturdy one.

Rachel – You are not just my sister, but one of my best friends. Your encouragement has been a constant source of strength. I can always count on you to show up when it matters most. You never hesitate to pick up the phone when I need to talk, and your loyalty and sense of humor make everything brighter. I know you love to tease me about spending time in my morning quiet time, but you always give me the time I need, understanding the value it brings to me. You see the fruit it bears, and that means the world. You've always been in my corner, and I'm so grateful for that. Thank you for being the amazing person you are.

Grandma and Grandpap – Thank you for showing me what it looks like to follow Jesus. We didn't have to talk about Him for me to see Him in you. Your warm hospitality, radical generosity, and the fullness of your prayer lives matters so much, and I noticed it. I noticed from a very young age that the atmosphere shifted when I was with you. As an adult, I realize it's because you showed me in every interaction what it looks like to truly be the hands and feet of Jesus. I am confident that I am who I am, where I am, and doing the things I'm doing today because of the prayers you've prayed and the seeds you've sown within me.

Nana and Grandpa – Thank you for prioritizing family. Every time I look around our giant holiday table, I see a picture of the Kingdom of God. I grew up knowing that you had an open-door policy, and that your table always had room for more (if not physically, you'd make room!). We started holiday meals with gratitude and ended them by taking food to your neighbors. There is something special about being together–not just on holidays, but for vacations and other special occasions too. Thank you for making that the standard. I grew up thinking everyone did that. It didn't occur to me until later that I was just one of the lucky ones.

The Johnson Family – Thank you for welcoming me into your hearts and your home. Thank you for your unwavering support, for celebrating with me throughout this process, and for believing that God will use this book to do something meaningful. Thank you for trusting me to be a voice, a role model, and a friend to your children. My life is so much richer because of each of you. Thank you for being, and for creating, spaces of joy, warmth, and belonging. What a gift it is to be your friend.

To my Beta Readers: Stacey, Kelly, Kory and Beth – AKA, my amazing friends who read through this work to make sure it was the absolute best it could be. Thank you! Your thorough feedback, thoughtful questions, and detailed edits helped to pull out of me the very best I had to offer. You helped transform this work into something lightyears better than I could have ever imagined.

Stacey – the level of effort you dedicated to reading through this manuscript did not go unnoticed. I deeply appreciate the way you prioritized this in a season where there are so many other ways you could have spent your time. Your attention to detail and your willingness to challenge me took this book up a notch. The work God did in my heart that eventually led to this book started when you took me under your wing and began the difficult and time-consuming task of leading and discipling me. I am profoundly grateful that anyone who picks up this book gets to read the version with your fingerprints on it, and gets to experience the version of me who was guided closer to Jesus through you.

Kelly – I can't thank you enough for the ways you encouraged and prayed this project into being. From the early days of joking about me "someday" writing a book to the heartfelt conversations about the good and the hard things God was teaching me (so much of which is in this book), you've been there through it all. You've shown me time and time again that what I was learning in Scripture and wrestling with in prayer mattered beyond myself and that maybe there were others who could benefit from my vulnerability. Thank you for reading this, over and over, and giving your thoughtful input. This book is better because of you. I am better because of you.

Kory – thank you for choosing to spend precious moments reading this book while you were home with my newest mini BFF, your sweet newborn son. The unique lens you brought to this helped me to see things in new ways. Your frequent encouragement helped spur me on to cross the finish line. You were truly one of my loudest cheerleaders. I have long admired your depth of faith and your willingness to cling to Him. So, for you to point out parts of this book that mattered most to you held so much weight.

Beth – You may never know this side of heaven the impact you've had on me. Our "heart dumps," as you so lovingly called them in the beautiful foreword you wrote, propelled me into the level of vulnerability and curiosity necessary to bring this book to life. You are one of the few who not only understand the joys, tears, doubts, fears, and moments of celebration that came with writing this book, but you were also there when the very content of this book was being placed on my heart. You provided a safe space for me to wonder out loud, and with compassion, you wondered alongside me. Your wise counsel has shaped me, and I'm confident that your prayers over the years have brought about meaningful shifts in my life and my future—some of which I'm aware of and others I may never fully comprehend. Thank you for your friendship, your grace, and your wisdom. Thank you for holding hope with me. Thank you for believing with me and for me, for the realization of this book and the impact God could have through these pages, and for so many other dreams to come. I am so humbled by your foreword and honored that the first words people will read are yours. You so gracefully invite readers into this book in a way I believe will make them feel held–as if they are settling into a safe space. You have cracked open your heart so they will trust mine. What a gift. You are a radiant light, my friend. Keep on shining.

To my Fairy God Kids — You two bring a fullness to my life that I didn't even know was possible. I am so grateful for your friendship! I admire your silliness, joy, creativity, thoughtfulness, courage, curiosity, and so much more! You bring out all the very best parts of me. These pages are dedicated to you, and I pray that someday they could be a resource to help you continue to know and love the God who perfectly created you and Who earnestly pursues you. The responsibility I hold as your friend to continue passionately following Jesus, letting Him shape me, and trying my best to love Him and to love you well matters deeply to me. I promise that I will do that as wholeheartedly as I can. Thank you for being you and for sharing your hearts and your lives with me. I am a better person because of you.

Amy Seiffert — my sweet writing coach... "thank you" doesn't really feel weighty enough, but thank you! You stuck with me when I was fumbling around trying to figure out this nudge towards writing when I had never considered writing before. You stuck with me as I navigated how vulnerable I should be in my writing, how to manage my time, and how to figure out what I should even write about. You watched as the idea for this book came alive as I excitedly shared about this prayer journal I created for myself and the themes that were arising. When I watched your face light up and subsequently point out that I, too, was smiling from ear to ear, we both knew at that moment that I landed on something special. Thank you for all of the wisdom and guidance you imparted to me as someone who not only has "been there, done that" but who has made a beautiful career out of serving Jesus and loving His children (big and small) as an author, speaker, coach, parent, spouse, and friend. You so wildly and successfully interweave your own experiences with the Truth in God's word in a way that is so tangible, relatable, and authentic. Thank you for sharing your gifts with me and coaching me along the way. This book surely would not be entering anyone's hands if not for you.

The Hope*Books Team: Brian, Hope, Abby, Rachel, and so many more—Thank you for taking a chance on me and helping me get these hope-filled words out to people who need them. Regardless of how far-reaching this work becomes or where these words take me, my obedience mattered, and your expertise helped my "yes" to Jesus be fulfilled. Thank you for all of your support, guidance, tools, and for the countless team members behind the scenes that made this possible. I am grateful to be a Hope*Books Author.

Author Bio

MEGAN CARLTON is a lifelong learner and knowledge seeker. With a deep love for God and a nurturing spirit, she brings her own experiences struggling with identity and purpose to life in a way that offers hope and a workable process for others. Megan is a night owl turned morning person through a call to 4:30 am quiet time and has used that time with God to personally work through and subsequently document her identity journey with the Lord. She currently resides in the Greater Cincinnati area, where she has made it her personal goal to find the best tacos in the city.